A

FRAGMENT

ON

GOVERNMENT;

OR, A

𝕮𝖔𝖒𝖒𝖊𝖓𝖙 𝖔𝖓 𝖙𝖍𝖊 𝕮𝖔𝖒𝖒𝖊𝖓𝖙𝖆𝖗𝖎𝖊𝖘:

BEING

AN EXAMINATION OF WHAT IS DELIVERED ON THE
SUBJECT OF GOVERNMENT IN GENERAL, IN THE
INTRODUCTION TO SIR WILLIAM BLACKSTONE'S
COMMENTARIES: WITH A PREFACE, IN
WHICH IS GIVEN A CRITIQUE ON
THE WORK AT LARGE.

BY

JEREMY BENTHAM, ESQ.

OF LINCOLN'S-INN.

'Rien ne recule plus le progrès des connoissances, qu'un mauvais ouvrage d'un
Auteur célèbre : parce qu'avant d'instruire, il faut commencer par detromper.'
Montesquieu Esprit des Loix, L. XXX. Ch. XV.

SECOND EDITION, ENLARGED.

LONDON:

PRINTED FOR E. WILSON, ROYAL EXCHANGE; AND
W. PICKERING, LINCOLN'S-INN FIELDS.

CONTENTS.

CONTENTS.

CHAP. I.

CONTENTS.

CONTENTS.

CONTENTS.

CHAP. III.

CHAP. IV.

CONTENTS.

CHAP. V.

List of such of the works of JEREMY BENTHAM, *as are in print, set down in the order of their dates, (which may be procured of the publishers of this work). Those marked* * *have been published, but are out of print. Those marked* ‖ *have never yet been published.*

---

1. Fragment on Government; or, a Comment on the Commentaries : being a Critique on some passages in Blackstone's Commentaries. Anonymous. Anno. 1776. 8vo. pp. 265—republished 1823.

2. View of the Hard Labour Bill, with Observations relative to Penal Jurisprudence in general. 1778. 8vo. pp. 114. price 3s.

3. Defence of Usury, 12mo. First Edition, 1787. Third Edition, published in 12mo. with Second Edition of Protest against Law Taxes. 1817. Price 7s.

4. Introduction to the Principles of Morals and Legislation, 1789. 4to.—republished 1823. 2 vols. 8vo.

5. Panopticon: or the Inspection-House: containing the idea of a new principle of Construction applicable to any sort of Establishment, in which persons of any description are to be kept under Inspection; and in particular to Penitentiary Houses, Prisons, Houses of Industry, Work-Houses, Poor-Houses, Manufactories, Mad-Houses, Lazarettos, Hospitals, and Schools; with a Plan of Management adapted to the principle, 1791, 2 vols. 8vo. Price 14s.

6. Draught of a Code for the Organization of the Judicial Establishment in France: with Critical Observations on the Draught proposed by the National Assembly Committee, in the form of a perpetual Commentary, 1790 or 1791, 8vo. 242 pages very closely printed.‖

7. Essay on Political Tactics: containing six of the principal Rules proper to be observed by a Political Assembly, in the process of forming a Decision; with the Reasons on which they are grounded; and a comparative application of them to British and French practice: being a Fragment of a larger Work; a sketch of which is subjoined, 1791, 4to. pp. 64.‖

8. Emancipate your Colonies: an Address (thus intituled) by Jeremy Bentham to the National Assembly of France, 1793, 8vo. pp. 48. "Your Pre-"decessors made me a French Citizen: hear me speak like one," &c.‖

9. Supply without Burthen; or, Escheat *vice* Taxation: published with 1st. Edition of Protest against Law Taxes, 1796, small 8vo. or 12mo.

10. Pauper Management: a Letter on the Situation and Relief of the Poor: addressed to Mr. Arthur Young, Editor of the Annals of Agriculture, and published in that Work, 1797, 8vo. pp. 288, with Tables.

11. Letters to Lord Pelham, &c. &c. &c. "giving a comparative View of "the System of Penal Colonization in New South Wales, and the Home Pe-"nitentiary System, prescribed by two Acts of Parliament of the Years 1794 "and 1799;" viz. in consequence of an acceptance given to a Proposal of the Author's, grounded on the Plan delineated in *Panopticon* as above, 1802, 8vo.‖

12. Plea for the Constitution, 1803; written in continuation of the above.‖

13. Introduction to the Rationale of Evidence, pp. 148.‖

14. Scotch Reform, compared with English Non-Reform; in a series of Letters to Lord Grenville. 1806. 8vo. pp. 100 closely printed: relative to the Judicial Establishment in Scotland and England. Price 6s.

15. Elements of the Art of Packing, as applied to Special Juries: particularly in cases of Libel-Law, 8vo. pp. 269, printed 1810, published 1821, Effingham Wilson, Royal Exchange, price 10s. 6d.

16. *Swear not at all;*" containing an exposure of the Needlessness and Mischievousness, as well as Anti-christianity of the ceremony of an Oath: with proof of the abuses of it, especially in the University of Oxford. Printed 1813: published 1817, pp. 97. 8vo. price 3s. 6d.

17. Table of Springs of Action: printed anno 1815: published anno 1817. 8vo. price 2s.

18. Defence of Economy against Edmund Burke; (written 1810) published in the Pamphleteer, No. XVI. January, 1817, 8vo. pp. 47.

19. Defence of Economy against the Right Honourable George Rose. (written 1810) published in the Pamphleteer, No. XVIII. January, 1817, pp. 52.

20. Chrestomathia, Part I. explanatory of a proposed School for the extension of the new System of Instruction to the higher branches of learning, for the use of the middling and higher ranks of life, 1816, 8vo. Part II. being an Essay on Nomenclature and Classification; including a critical examination of the Encyclopedical Table of Lord Bacon, as improved by D'Alembert; 1817. With Tables. 8vo. Price 15s.

21. Plan of Parliamentary Reform, with reasons for each Article; and an Introduction, shewing the necessity of radical, and the inadequacy of moderate Reform; 1817. 8vo. Price 8s.*

Another Edition, with Notes and Alterations, by permission of the Author, by T. J. Wooler. Price 5s.

22. Bentham's radical Reform Bill, with extracts from the reasons, 1819. Effingham Wilson, Royal Exchange. Price 4s.

23. Papers relative to Codification and Public Instruction; including Correspondence with the Emperor Alexander, and the President and divers other Constituted Authorities of the American United States, 1817, 8vo. Price 8s.

24. Church-of-Englandism and its Catechism examined; preceded by Strictures on the Exclusionary System, as pursued in the National Society's Schools; interspersed with parallel views of the English and Scottish Established Churches; and concluding with Remedies Proposed for Abuses Indicated; and an Examination of the Parliamentary System of Church Reform lately pursued, and still pursuing; including the Proposed New Churches. Effingham Wilson, Royal Exchange, 8vo. pp. 794, mostly very closely printed. Price 20s.

25. The King against Edmunds and others; set down for trial at Warwick, on the 29th of March, 1820. Brief Remarks tending to shew the untena-

26. The King against Sir Charles Wolseley, baronet, and Joseph Harrison, schoolmaster; set down for trial at Chester, on the 4th of April, 1820. Brief Remarks tending to shew the untenability of this indictment, 1820, pp. 39, 8vo.||

27. The Liberty of the Press and Public Discussion, 1821. pp. 38, 8vo. Price 1s.

28. Three tracts relative to Spanish and Portuguese affairs, with a continual eye to English ones. I. On a House of Lords. II. On Judicial Delays. III. On Antiquated Constitutions. 1821.

29. Observations on the Restrictive and Prohibitory Commercial System, especially with a reference to the decree of the Spanish Cortes of July, 1820.
" Leave us alone."
From the MSS. of Jeremy Bentham, esq. By John Bowring. Effingham Wilson, Royal Exchange, 8vo. Price 2s.

30. Letters to the Count Toreno, on the proposed Penal Code, delivered in by the Legislative Committee of the Spanish Cortes, April 25, 1821, written at the Court's request, 1822. Effingham Wilson, Royal Exchange. Price 5s.

List of Works published at different times in French by MR. DUMONT *of Geneva, from unfinished papers of* JEREMY BENTHAM.

" 1. Traités de Législation Civile et Pénale, précédés de Principes Géné-
" raux de Législation, et d'une Vue d'un Corps complet de Droits; terminés
" par un Essai sur l'Influence des tems et des lieux relativement aux lois.
" Paris, 1802. 3 tomes."

" 2. Théorie des Peines et des Récompenses. Londres, 1811. 2 tomes."

" 3. Essai sur la Tactique des Assemblées Politiques.   Genève, 1816;
' ensemble, sur les Sophismes."

** Of No. 1, 3000 sold: Second Edition of all three published at Paris.

PREFACE

TO THE FIRST EDITION PUBLISHED IN 1776.

THE age we live in is a busy age; in which know- *Motives of the present undertaking.* ledge is rapidly advancing towards perfection. In the natural world, in particular, every thing teems with discovery and with improvement. The most distant and recondite regions of the earth traversed and explored—the all-vivifying and subtle element of the air so recently analyzed and made known to us,—are striking evidences, were all others want- ing, of this pleasing truth.

Correspondent to *discovery* and *improvement* in the natural world, is *reformation* in the moral: if that which seems a common notion be, indeed, a true one, that in the moral world there no longer remains any matter for *discovery*. Perhaps, how- ever, this may not be the case: perhaps among such observations as would be best calculated to serve as grounds for reformation, are some which, being observations of matters of fact hitherto either incompletely noticed, or not at all, would, when produced, appear capable of bearing the name of discoveries: with so little method and precision

b

of
·nt
:ing. have the consequences of this fundamental axiom, *it is the greatest happiness of the greatest number that is the measure of right and wrong,* been as yet developed.

Be this as it may, if there be room for making, and if there be use in publishing, *discoveries* in the *natural* world, surely there is not much less room for making, nor much less use in proposing, *reformation* in the *moral.* If it be a matter of importance and of use to us to be made acquainted with *distant* countries, surely it is not a matter of much less importance, nor of much less use to us, to be made better and better acquainted with the chief means of living happily in our *own:* If it be of importance and of use to us to know the principles of the element we breathe, surely it is not of much less importance nor of much less use to comprehend the principles, and endeavour at the improvement of those *laws,* by which alone we breathe it in security. If to this endeavour we should fancy any Author, especially any Author of great name, to *be,* and as far as could in such case be expected, to *avow himself* a determined and persevering enemy, what should we say of him? We should say that the interests of reformation, and through them the welfare of mankind, were inseparably connected with the downfall of his works: of a great part, at least, of the esteem and influence which these works might under whatever title have acquired.

Such an enemy it has been my misfortune (and not mine only) to see, or fancy at least I saw, in the Author of the celebrated COMMENTARIES *on the* LAWS *of* ENGLAND: an Author whose works have had beyond comparison a more extensive circulation, have obtained a greater share of esteem, of applause, and consequently of influence (and that by a title on many grounds so indisputable) than any other writer who on that subject has ever yet appeared.

Motives of the present undertaking.

It is on this account that I conceived, some time since, the design of pointing out some of what appeared to me the capital blemishes of that work, particularly this grand and fundamental one, the antipathy to reformation; or rather, indeed, of laying open and exposing the universal inaccuracy and confusion which seemed to my apprehension to pervade the whole. For, indeed, such an ungenerous antipathy seemed of itself enough to promise a general vein of obscure and crooked reasoning, from whence no clear and sterling knowledge could be derived; so intimate is the connexion between some of the gifts of the understanding, and some of the affections of the heart.

History of it.

It is in this view then that I took in hand that part of the first volume to which the Author has given the name of INTRODUCTION. It is in this part of the work that is contained whatever comes under the denomination of *general principles*. It is

t. in this part of the work that are contained such preliminary views as it seemed proper to him to give of certain objects real or imaginary, which he found connected with his subject Law by identity of name: two or three sorts of Laws of *Nature*, the *revealed* Law, and a certain Law of *Nations*. It is in this part of the work that he has touched upon several topics which relate to all laws or institutions [a] in general, or at least to whole classes of institutions without relating to any one more than to another.

To speak more particularly, it is in this part of his work that he has given a definition, such as it is, of that whole branch of law which he had taken for his subject; that branch, which some, considering it as a main stock, would term Law without addition; and which he, to distinguish it from those others its *condivident branches* [b], terms law *municipal*:—an account, such as it is, of the nature and origin of *Natural* Society the mother, and of *Political* Society the daughter, of Law *municipal*, duly begotten in the bed of Metaphor:—a division, such as it is, of *a* law, individually considered, into what he fancies to be its *parts*:—an account, such as it is, of the method to be taken for *interpreting* any law that may occur.

[a] I add here the word *institutions*, for the sake of including rules of *Common* Law, as well as portions of *Statute* Law.

[b] *Membra condividentia*—SAUND. Log. L. I. c. 46.

In regard to the Law of England in particular, it H is here that he gives an account of the division of it into its two branches (branches, however, that are no ways distinct in the purport of them, when once established, but only in respect of the source from whence their establishment took its rise) the *Statute* or *Written* law, as it is called, and the *Common* or *Unwritten* :—an account of what are called *General Customs*, or institutions in force throughout the whole empire, or at least the whole nation;—of what are called *Particular Customs*, institutions of local extent established in particular districts; and of such *adopted* institutions of a general extent, as are parcel of what are called the *Civil* and the *Canon* laws; all three in the character of so many branches of what is called the *Common Law:*—in fine, a general account of *Equity*, that capricious and incomprehensible mistress of our fortunes, whose features neither our Author, nor perhaps any one is well able to delineate;—of *Equity*, who having in the beginning been a rib of *Law*, but since in some dark age plucked from her side, when sleeping, by the hands not so much of God as of enterprizing Judges, now lords it over her parent sister :—

All this, I say, together with an account of the different districts of the empire over which different portions of the Law prevail, or over which the Law has different degrees of force, composes that part of our Author's work which he has styled the IN-

t. TRODUCTION. His eloquent " Discourse on the " study of the Law," with which, as being a discourse of the rhetorical kind rather than of the didactic, I proposed not to intermeddle, prefaces the whole.

It would have been in vain to have thought of travelling over the whole of so vast a work. My design, therefore, was to take such a portion of it, as might afford a fair and adequate specimen of the character and complexion of the whole. For this purpose the part here marked out would, I thought, abundantly suffice. This, however narrow in extent, was the most conspicuous, the most characteristic part of our Author's work, and that which was most his own. The rest was little more than compilation. Pursuing my examination thus far, I should pursue it, I thought, as far as was necessary for my purpose : and I had little stomach to pursue a task at once so laborious and so invidious any farther. If *Hercules*, according to the old proverb, is to be known *ex pede;* much more, thought I, is he to be known *ex capite.*

In these views it was that I proceeded as far as the middle of the definition of Law *municipal.* It was there I found, not without surprize, the digression which makes the subject of the present essay. This threw me at first into no small perplexity. To give no account of it at all;—to pass wholly *sub silentio,* so large, and in itself so material a part of

the work I was examining, would seem strange : at
the same time I saw no possibility of entering into
an examination of a passage so anomalous, without
cutting in pieces the thread of the discourse. Under this doubt I determined at any rate, for the
present, to pass it by; the rather as I could not
perceive any connexion that it had with any thing
that came before or after. I did so; and continuing my examination of the definition from which it
digressed, I travelled on to the end of the Introduction. It then became necessary to come to some
definitive resolution concerning this eccentric part
of it: and the result was, that being loth to leave
the enterprize I had begun in this respect imperfect, I sat down to give what I intended should be
a very slight and general survey of it. The farther,
however, I proceeded in examining it, the more
confused and unsatisfactory it appeared 'to me:
and the greater difficulty I found in knowing what
to make of it, the more words it cost me, I found,
to say so. In this way, and by these means it was
that the present Essay grew to the bulk in which
the Reader sees it. When it was nearly completed,
it occurred to me, that as the digression itself
which I was examining was perfectly distinct from,
and unconnected with the text from which it starts,
so was, or so at least might be, the *critique* on that
digression, from the *critique* on the text. The former was by much too large to be engrafted into

History of it. the latter: and since if it accompanied it at all, it could only be in the shape of an Appendix, there seemed no reason why the same publication should include them both. To the former, therefore, as being the least, I determined to give that finish which I was able, and which I thought was necessary: and to publish it in this detached manner, as the first, if not the only part of a work, the principal and remaining part of which may possibly see the light some time or other, under some such title as that of " *A* COMMENT *on the* COMMENTARIES."

In the mean time that I may stand more fully justified, or excused at least, in an enterprize to most perhaps so extraordinary, and to many doubtless so unacceptable, it may be of use to endeavour to state with some degree of precision, the grounds of that war which, for the interests of true science, and of liberal improvement, I think myself bound to wage against this work. I shall therefore proceed to mark out and distinguish those points of view in which it seems principally reprehensible, not forgetting those in which it seems still entitled to our approbation and applause.

The business of the *Censor* distinguished from that of the *Expositor.* There are two characters, one or other of which every man who finds any thing to say on the subject of Law, may be said to take upon him;—that of the *Expositor,* and that of the *Censor.* To the province of the *Expositor* it belongs to explain to us what, as he supposes, the Law *is:* to that of the

Censor, to observe to us what he thinks it *ought to* *be*. The former, therefore, is principally occupied in stating, or in enquiring after *facts :* [c] the latter, in discussing *reasons*. The *Expositor*, keeping within his sphere, has no concern with any other faculties of the mind than the *apprehension*, the *memory*, and the *judgment :* the latter, in virtue of those sentiments of pleasure or displeasure which he finds occasion to annex to the objects under his review, holds some intercourse with the *affections*. That which *is* Law, is, in different countries, widely different : while that which *ought to be*, is in all countries to a great degree the same. The *Expositor*, therefore, is always the citizen of this or that particular country : the *Censor* is, or ought to be the citizen of the world. To the *Expositor* it belongs to shew what the *Legislator* and his underworkman the *Judge* have done *already :* to the *Censor* it belongs to suggest what the *Legislator ought* to do *in future*. To the Censor, in short, it belongs to *teach* that science, which when by change of hands converted into an *art*, the LEGISLATOR *practises*.

[c] In practice, the question of *Law* has commonly been spoken of as opposed to that of *fact* : but this distinction is an accidental one. That a Law commanding or prohibiting such a *sort* of action, has been established, is as much a *fact*, as that an *individual* action of that sort has been committed. The establishment of a Law may be spoken of as a *fact*, at least for the purpose of distinguishing it from any consideration that may be offered as a *reason* for such Law.

The latter alone our Author's.

Let us now return to our Author. Of these two perfectly distinguishable functions, the latter alone is that which it fell necessarily within his province to discharge. His professed object was to explain to us what the Laws of England *were*. " *Ita lex* " *scripta est*," was the only motto which he stood engaged to keep in view. The work of *censure* (for to this word, in default of any other, I find it necessary to give a *neutral* sense) the work of *censure*, as it may be styled, or, in a certain sense, of *criticism*, was to him but a *parergon*—a work of supererogation: a work, indeed, which, if aptly executed, could not but be of great ornament to the principal one, and of great instruction as well as entertainment to the Reader, but from which our Author, as well as those that had gone before him on the same line, might, without being chargeable with any deficiency, have stood excused: a work which, when superadded to the principal, would lay the Author under additional obligations, and impose on him new duties: which, notwithstanding whatever else it might differ in from the principal one, agrees with it in this, that it ought to be executed with impartiality, or not at all.

Laws ought to be scrutinized with freedom.

If, on the one hand, a hasty and undiscriminating condemner of what is established, may expose himself to contempt; on the other hand, a bigotted or corrupt defender of the works of power, becomes guilty, in a manner, of the abuses which he supports : the more so if, by oblique glances and sophistical glosses, he studies to guard from reproach, or recommend to favour, what. he knows not how, and dares not attempt, to justify. To a man who contents himself with simply stating an institution as he thinks it *is*, no share, it is plain, can justly be attributed (nor would any one think of attributing to him any share) of whatever reproach, any more than of whatever applause the institution may be thought to merit. But if not content with this humbler function, he takes upon him to give *reasons* in behalf of it, reasons whether *made* or found by him, it is far otherwise. Every false and sophistical reason that he contributes to circulate, he himself is chargeable with: nor ought he to be holden guiltless even of such as, in a work where *fact* not *reason* is the question he delivers as from other writers without censure. By officiously adopting them he makes them his own, though delivered under the names of the respective Authors : not much less than if delivered under his own. For the very idea of a *reason* betokens approbation : so that to deliver a remark under that character, and that without censure, is to adopt it. A man will scarcely, therefore, without some note of disapprobation, be the instrument of introducing, in the guise of a reason, an argument which he does not really wish to.see approved. Some method or other he will take to wash his hands of it : some

Laws ought to be scrutinized with freedom. method or other he will take to let men see that what he means to be understood to do, is merely to report the judgment of another, not to pass one of his own. Upon that other then he will lay the blame: at least he will take care to repel it from himself. If he omits to do this, the most favourable cause that can be assigned to the omission is indifference: indifference to the public welfare—that indifference which is itself a crime.

It is wonderful how forward some have been to look upon it as a kind of presumption and ingratitude, and rebellion, and cruelty, and I know not what besides, not to allege only, nor to own, but to suffer any one so much as to imagine, that an old-established law could in any respect be a fit object of condemnation. Whether it has been a kind of *personification* that has been the cause of this, as if the Law were a living creature, or whether it has been the mechanical veneration for antiquity, or what other delusion of the fancy, I shall not here enquire. For my part, I know not for what good reason it is that the merit of justifying a law when right should have been thought greater, than that of censuring it when wrong. Under a government of Laws, what is the motto of a good citizen? *To obey punctually; to censure freely.*

Thus much is certain; that a system that is never to be censured, will never be improved: that if nothing is ever to be found fault with, nothing will ever be mended : and that a resolution to justify Laws ought to be scrutinized with freedom. every thing at any rate, and to disapprove of nothing, is a resolution which, pursued in future, must stand as an effectual bar to all the *additional* happiness we can ever hope for ; pursued hitherto would have robbed us of that share of happiness which we enjoy already.

Nor is a disposition to find "every thing as it "should be," less at variance with itself, than with reason and utility. The common-place arguments in which it vents itself justify not what is established, in effect any more than they condemn it; since whatever *now* is establishment, *once* was innovation.

Precipitate censure, cast on a political institution, does but recoil on the head of him who casts it. From such an attack it is not the institution itself, if well grounded, that can suffer. What a man says against it either makes impression or makes none. If none, it is just as if nothing had been said about the matter; if it *does* make an impression, it naturally calls up some one or other in defence. For if the institution is in truth a beneficial one to the community in general, it cannot but have given an interest in its preservation to a number of individuals. By their industry, then, the reasons on which it is grounded are brought to light ; from the observation of which those who acquiesced in it before upon trust, now embrace it upon conviction. Censure, therefore, though ill-founded, has no other effect upon an institution than to bring it to that test, by which the value of those, indeed, on which prejudice alone has stamped a currency, is cried down, but by which the credit of those of sterling utility is confirmed.

Nor is it by any means from passion and ill-humour, that censure, passed upon legal institutions, is apt to take its birth. When it is from passion and ill-humour that men speak, it is with *men* that they are in ill-humour, not with laws; it is men, not laws, that are the but of " arrogance." [*d*] Spleen and turbulence may indeed prompt men to

[*d*] " *Arrogance* ;" our Author calls it " *the utmost arrogance**, to " censure what has, at least, a better chance to be right, than the " singular notions of any particular man :" meaning thereby certain ecclesiastical institutions. Vibrating, as it should seem, between passion and discretion, he has thought it necessary, indeed, to insert in the sentence that, which being inserted, turns it into nothing : After the word " censure," " with contempt" he adds, " and rude-" ness :" as if there needed a professor to inform us, that to treat any thing with contempt and rudeness is arrogance. " Indecency," he had already called it, " to set up private judgment in opposition " to public ;" and this without restriction, qualification, or reserve. This was in the first transport of a holy zeal, before discretion had come in to his assistance. This passage the Doctors *Priestly*† and *Furneaux*‡, who, in quality of Dissenting Ministers, and champions of dissenting opinions, saw themselves particularly attacked in it, have not suffered to pass unnoticed; any more than has the celebrated Author of the " *Remarks on the Acts of the* 13*th Parlia-* " *ment* §," who found it adverse to his enterprize, for the same

* 4 Comm. p. 50.   † See Remarks, &c.

‡ See Letters to Mr. Justice Blackstone, 1771. Second Edition;
§ In the Preface.

quarrel with living individuals; but when they Laws ought to be scrutinised with freedom. make complaint of the dead letter of the Law, the work of departed lawgivers, against whom no personal antipathy can have subsisted, it is always from the observation, or from the belief at least, of some real grievance. The Law is no man's enemy; the Law is no man's rival. Ask the clamorous and unruly multitude—it is never the Law itself that is in the wrong; it is always some wicked interpreter of the Law that has corrupted and abused it. [e].

reason that is hostile to every other liberal plan of political discussion.

⁎ My edition of the Commentaries happens to be the first: since the above paragraph was written I have been directed to a later. In this later edition the passage about "indecency" is, like the other about "arrogance," explained away into nothing. What we are now told is, that "to set up private judgment in [*virulent* "*and factious*] opposition to public *authority*" (he might have added—or to *private* either) is "indecency." [See the 5th Edit. 8vo. p. 50, as in the 1st.] This we owe, I think, to Dr. Furneaux. The Doctors Furneaux and Priestly, under whose well-applied correction our Author has smarted so severely, have a good deal to answer for: They have been the means of his adding a good deal of this kind of rhetorical lumber to the plentiful stock there was of it before. One passage, indeed, a passage deep-tinctured with religious gall, they have been the means of clearing away entirely *; and in this, at least, they have done good service. They have made him sophisticate; they have made him even expunge; but all the Doctors in the world, I doubt, would not bring him to confession. See his Answer to Dr. Priestly.

[e] There is only one way in which censure, cast upon the Laws,

* See Furneaux, Letter VII.

Laws ought to
be scrutinized
with freedom.
Thus destitute of foundation are the terrors, or
pretended terrors, of those who shudder at the idea
of a free censure of established institutions. So
little does the peace of society require the aid of
those lessons which teach men to accept of any
thing as a reason, and to yield the same abject and
indiscriminating homage to the Laws here, which is
paid to the despot elsewhere. The fruits of such
tuition are visible enough in the character of that
race of men who have always occupied too large
a space in the circle of the profession; A passive
and enervate race, ready to swallow any thing,
and to acquiesce in any thing; with intellects incapable of distinguishing right from wrong, and with
affections alike indifferent to either; insensible,
short-sighted, obstinate; lethargic, yet liable to be
driven in convulsions by false terrors; deaf to the

has a greater tendency to do harm than good; and that is when it
sets itself to contest their validity; I mean, when abandoning the
question of expediency, it sets itself to contest the right. But this
is an attack to which old-established Laws are not so liable. As
this is the last though but too common resource of passion and ill-
humour; and what men scarce think of betaking themselves to,
unless irritated by personal competitions, it is that to which recent
Laws are most exposed. I speak of what are called *written* Laws;
for as to *unwritten* institutions, as there is no such thing as any
certain symbol by which their authority is attested, *their* validity,
how deeply rooted soever, is what we see challenged without re-
morse. A radical weakness, interwoven into the very constitution
of all unwritten Law.

voice of reason and public utility; obsequious only to the whisper of interest, and to the beck of power.

This head of mishchief, perhaps, is no more than what may seem included under the former. For why is it an evil to a country that the minds of those who have the Law under their management should be thus enfeebled? It is because it finds them impotent to every enterprize of improvement.

Not that a race of lawyers and politicians of this enervate breed is much less dangerous to the duration of that share of felicity which the state possesses at any given period, than it is mortal to its chance of attaining to a greater. If the designs of a Minister are inimical to his country, what is the man of all others for him to make an instrument of or a dupe? Of all men, surely none so fit as that sort of man who is ever on his knees before the footstool of Authority, and who, when those *above* him, or *before* him, have pronounced, thinks it a crime to have an opinion of his own.

Those who duly consider upon what slight and trivial circumstances, even in the happiest times, the adoption or rejection of a Law so often turns; circumstances with which the utility of it has no imaginable connection—those who consider the desolate and abject state of the human intellect, during the periods in which so great a part of the still subsisting mass of institutions had their birth— those who consider the backwardness there is in

Laws ought to be scrutinized with freedom. most men, unless when spurred by personal interests or resentments, to run-a-tilt against the Colossus of authority—those, I say, who give these considerations their due weight, will not be quite so zealous, perhaps, as our Author has been to terrify men from setting up what is now " private judgment," against what once was " public :" [*f*] nor to thunder down the harsh epithet of " arrogance" on those, who, with whatever success, are occupied in bringing rude establishments to the test of polished reason. They will rather do what they can to cherish a disposition at once so useful and so rare : [*g*] which is so little connected with the causes that make popular discontentments dangerous, and which finds so little aliment in those propensities that govern the multitude of men. They will not be for giving such a turn to their discourses as to bespeak the whole of a man's favour for the defenders of what is established : nor all his resent-

[*f*] See note [*d*].

[*g*] One may well say *rare.* It is a matter of fact about which there can be no dispute. The truth of it may be seen in the multitude of *Expositors* which the Jurisprudence of every nation furnished, ere it afforded a single *Censor.* When Beccaria came, he was received by the intelligent as an Angel from heaven would be by the faithful. He may be styled the father of *Censorial Jurisprudence.* Montesquieu's was a work of the mixed kind. Before Montesquieu all was unmixed barbarism. Grotius and Puffendorf were to Censorial Jurisprudence what the Schoolmen were to Natural Philosophy.

ment for the assailants. They will acknowledge Laws ought to be scrutinized with freedom. that if there be some institutions which it is " arro- " gance" to attack, there may be others which it is effrontery to defend. TOURREIL [*h*] has defended torture : torture established by the " public judgment" of so many enlightened nations. BECCARIA ("indecent" and " arrogant" Beccaria!) has condemned it. Of these two, whose lot among men would one choose rather,—the Apologist's or the Censor's?

Of a piece with the discerment which enables a Our Author why attacked in the character of an Expositor. man to perceive, and with the courage which enables him to avow, the defects of a system of institutions, is that accuracy of conception which enables him to give a clear account of it. No wonder then, in a treatise partly of the *expository* class, and partly of the *censorial*, that if the latter department is filled with imbecility, symptoms of kindred weakness should characterize the former.

The former department, however, of our Author's work, is what, on its own account merely, I should scarce have found myself disposed to intermeddle with. The business of simple *exposition* is a harvest in which there seemed no likelihood of their being

---

[*h*] A French Jurist of the last age, whose works had like celebrity, and in many respects much the same sort of merits as our Author's. He was known to most advantage by a translation of Demosthenes. He is now forgotten.

Author attacked le charac- 'f an *Ex- tor.* any want of labourers : and into which therefore I had little ambition to thrust my sickle.

At any rate, had I sat down to make a report of it in this character alone, it would have been with feelings very different from those of which I now am conscious, and in a tone very different from that which I perceive myself to have assumed. In determining what conduct to observe respecting it, I should have considered whether the taint of error seemed to confine itself to parts, or to diffuse itself through the whole. In the latter case, the least invidious, and considering the bulk of the work, the most beneficial course would have been to have taken no notice of it at all, but to have sat down and tried to give a better. If not the whole in general, but scattered positions only had appeared exceptionable, I should have sat down to rectify those positions with the same. apathy with which they were advanced. To fall in an adverse way upon a work simply *expository*, if that were all there were of it, would have been alike ungenerous and unnecessary. In the involuntary errors of the *understanding* there can be little to excite, or at least to justify, resentment. That which alone, in a manner, calls for rigid censure, is the sinister bias of the *affections*. If then I may still continue to mention as separate, parts which in the work itself are so intimately, and, indeed, undistinguishably blended, it is the *censorial* part alone that has drawn from me that sort of animadversion I have been led to bestow indis- Our Author why attacked in the character of an *Expositor*. criminately on the whole. To lay open, and if possible supply, the imperfections of the *other*, is an operation that might indeed of itself do service; but that which I thought would do still more service, was the weakening the authority of *this*.

"Under the sanction of a great name every string of words however unmeaning, every opinion however erroneous, will have a certain currency. Reputation adds weight to sentiments from whence no part of it arose, and which had they stood alone might have drawn nothing, perhaps, but contempt. Popular fame enters not into nice distinctions. Merit in one department of letters affords a natural, and in a manner irrecusable presumption of merit in another, especially if the two departments be such between which their is apparently a close alliance.

Wonderful, in particular, is that influence which is gained over young minds, by the man who on account of whatever class of merit is esteemed in the character of a *preceptor*. Those who have derived, or fancy themselves to have derived knowledge from what he knows, or appears to know, will naturally be for judging as he judges; for reasoning as he reasons; for approving as he approves; for condemning as he condemns. On these accounts it is, that when the general complexion of a work is unsound, it may be of use to point an attack against the whole of it without distinction, although such

parts of it as are noxious as well as unsound be
only scattered here and there.

On these considerations then it may be of use to
shew, that the work before us, in spite of the merits
which recommend it so powerfully to the imagination and to the ear, has no better title on one
account than on another, to that influence which,
were it to pass unnoticed, it might continue to
exercise over the judgment.

The Introduction is the part to which, for reasons
that have been already stated, it was always my
intention to confine myself. It is but a part even of
this Introduction that is the subject of the present
Essay. What determined me to begin with this
small part of it is, the facility I found in separating
it from every thing that precedes or follows it. This
is what will be more particularly spoken to in
another place [i].

It is not that this part is among those which
seemed most open to animadversion. It is not that
stronger traces are exhibited in this part than in
another of that spirit in our Author which seems so
hostile to Reformation, and to that Liberty which is
Reformation's harbinger.

It is not here that he tramples on the right of
private judgment, that basis of every thing that an
Englishman holds dear [k]. It is not here, in par-

---

[i] See the ensuing Introduction.   [k] See note [a].

ticular, that he insults our understandings with nugatory reasons; stands forth the professed champion of religious intolerance; or openly sets his face against civil reformation.

It is not here, for example, he would persuade us, that a trader who occupies a booth at a fair is a *fool* for his pains; and on that account no fit object of the Law's protection [*l*].

It is not here that he gives the presence of *one* man at the *making* of a Law, as a *reason* why *ten thousand* others that are to *obey* it, need know nothing of the matter [*m*].

[*l*] " Burglary*," says our Author, " cannot be committed in a " tent or a booth erected in a market fair; though the owner may " lodge therein; *for* the Law regards thus highly nothing but per- " manent edifices; a house, or church; the wall, or gate of a town; " and it is the *folly* of the owner to lodge in so fragile a tenement." To save himself from this charge of folly, it is not altogether clear which of two things the trader ought to do; quit his business and not go to the fair at all: or leave his goods without any body to take care of them.

[*m*] Speaking of an Act of Parliament †, " There needs," he says, " no formal promulgation to give it the force of a Law, as was " necessary by the Civil Law with regard to the Emperor's Edicts; " *because* every man in England is, *in judgment of Law*, party to the " making of an Act of Parliament, being present thereat *by his re-* " *presentatives*." This, for ought I know, may be good *judgment of Law;* because any thing may be called judgment of Law, that comes from a Lawyer who has got a name: it seems, however, not much like any thing that can be called *judgment of common sense*.

* 4 Comm. Ch. XVI. p. 226.   † 1 Comm. Ch. II. p. 178.

Rreprehen-
sible passages
from the work
at large.

It is not here, that after telling us, in express
terms, there must be an "actual breaking" to make
burglary, he tells us, in the same breath, and in
terms equally express, where burglary may be
without actual breaking; and this *because* "the
" Law will not suffer itself to be trifled with [*n*]."

This notable piece of *astutia* was originally, I believe, judgment of
Lord Coke; it from thence became judgment of our Author: and
may have been judgment of more Lawyers than I know of before
and since. What grieves me is, to find many men of the best affections to a cause which needs no sophistry, bewildered and be-
wildering others with the like jargon.

[*n*] His words are *, " *There must be an actual breaking*, not a
" mere legal *clausum fregit* (by leaping over invisible ideal boun-
" daries, which may constitute a civil trespass) but a *substantial* and
" *forcible irruption.*" In the next sentence but two he goes on and
says,—" But to come down a chimney *is* held a burglarious entry;
" for that is as much closed as the nature of things will permit. So
" also to knock at a door, and upon opening it to rush in, with a fe-
" lonious intent; or under pretence of taking lodgings, to fall upon
" the landlord and rob him; or to procure a constable to gain ad-
" mittance, in order to search for traitors, and then to bind the con-
" stable and rob the house; *all these entries have been adjudged*
" *burglarious, though there was no actual breaking : for* the Law
will not suffer itself to be trifled with by such evasions."....Can it
be more egregiously trifled with than by such *reasons?*

I must own I have been ready to grow out of conceit with these
useful little particles, *for, because, since,* and others of that frater-
nity, from seeing the drudgery they are continually put to in these
Commentaries. The appearance of any of them is a sort of warning to me to prepare for some tautology, or some absurdity: for

* 4 Comm. Ch. XVI. p. 226.

It is not here, that after relating the Laws by
which peaceable Christians are made punishable for worshipping God according to their consciences, he pronounces with equal peremptoriness and complacency, that every thing, yes, " every thing is as " it should be [o]."

the same thing dished up over again in the shape of a reason for itself: or for a reason which, if a distinct one, is of the same stamp as those we have just seen. Other instances of the like hard treatment given to these poor particles will come under observation in the body of this essay. As to reasons of the first-mentioned class, of them one might pick out enough to fill a little volume.

[o] " In what I have now said," says he*, " I would not be " understood to derogate from the rights of the national Church, " or to favour a loose latitude of propagating any crude undigested " sentiments in religous matters. Of *propagating*, I say; for the " bare entertaining them, without an endeavour to diffuse them, " seems *hardly* cognizable by any human authority. I only mean " to illustrate the excellence of our present establishment, by " looking back to former times. *Every thing is now as it should* " *be:* unless, perhaps, that heresy ought to be more strictly " defined, and no prosecution permitted, even in the Ecclesiastical " Courts, till the tenets in question are by proper authority pre- " viously declared to be heretical. Under these restrictions it " seems *necessary* for the support of the national religion," (the national religion being such, we are to understand, as would not be able to support itself were any one at liberty to make objections to it) " that the officers of the Church should have power to censure " heretics, but not to exterminate or destroy them "

₀ Upon looking into a later edition (the fifth) I find this passage has undergone a modification. " After *Every thing is now*

* 4 Com. Ch. IV. p. 49.

It is not here, that he commands us to believe, and that on pain of forfeiting all pretensions to either "sense or probity," that the system of our jurisprudence is, in the whole and every part of it, the very quintessence of perfection [*p*].

as it should be," is added, " *with respect to the spiritual cognizance, and spiritual punishment of heresy.*" After " *the officers of the Church should have power to censure heretics,*" is added " *but not to harass them with temporal penalties, much less to exterminate or destroy them.*"

How far the mischievousness of the original text has been cured by this amendment, may be seen from Dr. Fúrneaux, Lett. II. p. 30, 2d edit.

[*p*] 1 Comm. 140. I would not be altogether positive, how far it was he meant this persuasion should extend itself in point of time; whether to those institutions only that happened to be in force at the individual instant of his writing : or whether to such opposite institutions also as, within any given distance of time from that instant, either *had* been in force, or were *about* to be.

His words are as follows ; " All these rights and liberties it is " our birthright to enjoy entire; unless where the Laws of our " country have laid them under necessary restraints. Restraints in " themselves so gentle and moderate, as will appear upon further " enquiry, that no man of *sense* or *probity* would wish to see them " slackened. For *all* of us have it in our choice to do *every thing* " that a *good* man would desire to do; and are restrained from " nothing, but what would be pernicious either to ourselves or our " fellow citizens."

If the Reader would know what these rights and liberties are, I answer him out of the same page, they are those, " in opposition " to one or other of which *every* species of compulsive tyranny and " oppression must act, having no other object upon which it can

It is not here that he assures us in point of fact, Reprehensible passages from the work at large. that there never *has* been an alteration made in the Law that men have not afterwards found reason to regret [*q*].

" *possibly* be employed." The liberty, for example, of worshipping God without being obliged to declare a belief in the XXXIX Articles, is a liberty that no "*good man*,"—" no man of sense or " probity," " would wish" for.

[*q*] 1 Comm. 70. If no reason can be found for an institution, we are to *suppose* one; and it is upon the strength of this supposed one we are to cry it up as reasonable: It is thus that the Law *is justified of her children.*

The words are—" Not that the particular reason of every rule " in the Law can, at this distance of time, be always precisely " assigned; but it is sufficient that there be nothing in the rule " *flatly* contradictory to reason, and then the Law will *presume* it to " be well founded. And it hath been an ancient observation in " the Laws of England," (he might with as good ground have added—*and in all other Laws*) " That whenever a standing rule, of " Law, of which the reason, perhaps, could not be remembered or " discerned, hath been [*wantonly*] broke in upon by *statutes* or *new* " *resolutions*, the wisdom of the rule hath in the end appeared from " the inconveniencies that have followed the innovation."

When a sentiment is expressed, and whether from caution, or from confusion of ideas, a clause is put in by way of qualifying it that turns it into nothing, in this case if we would form a fair estimate of the tendency and probable effect of the whole passage, the way is, I take it, to consider it as if no such clause were there. Nor let this seem strange. Taking the qualification into the account, the sentiment would make no impression on the mind at all; if it makes any, the qualification is dropped, and the mind is affected in the same manner nearly as it would be were the sentiment to stand unqualified.

Reprehen-
sible passages
from the work
at large.

It is not here that he turns the Law into a Castle,

This, I think, we may conclude to be the case with the passage
above-mentioned. The word "*wantonly*" is, in pursuance of our
Authors standing policy, put in by way of salvo. *With* it the
sentiment is as much as comes to nothing. *Without* it, it would be
extravagant. Yet in this extravagant form it is, probably, if in any,
that it passes upon the Reader.

The pleasant part of the contrivance is, the mentioning of
"*Statutes*" and "*Resolutions*" (Resolutions to wit, that is Decisions, of Courts of Justice) in the same breath; as if whether it
were by the one of them or the other, that a rule of Law was
broke in upon, made no difference. By a *Resolution* indeed, a
new Resolution, to break in upon a *standing* rule, is a practice that
in good truth is big with mischief. But this mischief on what does
it depend? Upon the *rule's* being a *reasonable* one? By no means:
but upon its being a *standing*, an established one. Reasonable
or not reasonable, is what makes comparatively but a trifling
difference.

A new resolution made in the teeth of an old-established rule is
mischievous—on what account? In that it puts men's expectations
universally to a fault, and shakes whatever confidence they may
have in the stability of any rules of Law, reasonable or not reasonable; that stability on which every thing that is valuable to a
man depends. Beneficial be it in ever so high a degree to the
party in whose favour it is made, the benefit it is of to *him* can
never be so great as to outweigh the mischief it is of to the community at large. Make the best of it, it is general evil for the sake
of partial good. It is what Lord Bacon calls setting the whole
house on fire, in order to roast one man's eggs.

Here then the *salvo* is not wanted; a " new resolution can never
" be acknowledged to be contrary to a standing rule," but it must
on that very account be acknowledged to be " *wanton.*" Let such
a resolution be made, and " inconveniencies" in abundance will

for the purpose of opposing every idea of "funda-
"mental" reparation [r].

sure enough ensue; and then will appear—what? not by any
means "the wisdom of the rule," but, what is a very different
thing, the folly of breaking in upon it.

It were almost superfluous to remark, that nothing of all this
applies in general to a statute; though particular Statutes may be
conceived that would thwart the course of expectation, and by that
means produce mischief in the same way in which it is produced
by irregular resolutions. A new statute, it is manifest, cannot,
unless it be simply a declaratory one, be made in any case, but it
must break in upon some standing rule of Law. With regard to
a Statute then to tell us that a "wanton" one has produced "incon-
" veniencies," what is it but to tell us that a thing that has been
mischievous has produced mischief?

Of this temper are the arguments of all those doating politicians,
who, when out of humour with a particular innovation without
being able to tell why, set themselves to declaim against all innovation, because it is innovation. It is the nature of owls to hate
the light: and it is the nature of those politicians who are wise by
rote, to detest every thing that forces them either to find (what,
perhaps, is impossible) reasons for a favourite persuasion, or (what
is not endurable) to discard it.

[r] 3 Comm. 268, at the end of Ch. XVII. which concludes
with three pages against Reformation. Our Author had better, perhaps, on this occasion, have kept clear of allegories: he should
have considered whether they might not be retorted on him with
severe retaliation. He should have considered, that it is not easier
to him to turn the Law into a Castle, than it is to the imagina-
tions of impoverished suitors to people it with Harpies. He should
have thought of the den of Cacus, to whose enfeebled optics, to
whose habits of dark and secret rapine, nothing was so hateful,
nothing so dangerous, as the light of day.

Reprehensi-
ble passages
from the
work at large.
It is not here that he turns with scorn upon those
beneficent Legislators, whose care it has been to
pluck the mask of Mystery from the face of Jurisprudence [s].

[s] 3 Comm. 322. It is from the decisions of Courts of Justice
that those rules of Law are framed, on the knowledge of which
depend the life, the fortune, the liberty of every man in the nation. Of these decisions the Records are, according to our Author [1 Comm. 71.] the most authentic histories. These Records
were, till within these five-and-forty years, in Law-Latin; a language which, upon a high computation, about one man in a thousand used to fancy himself to understand. In this Law-Latin it
is that our Author is satisfied they should have been continued,
because the pyramids of Egypt have stood longer than the tem-
ples of Palmyra. He observes to us, that the Latin language
could not express itself on the subject without borrowing a multitude of words from our own : which is to help to convince us that of
the two the former is the fittest to be employed. He gives us to
understand that, taking it altogether, there could be no room to
complain of it, seeing it was not more unintelligible than the jargon
of the schoolmen, some passages of which he instances ; and then
he goes on, " This technical Latin continued in use from the time
" of its first introduction till the subversion of our ancient constitu-
" tion under Cromwell ; when among many other innovations on
" the body of the Law, some for the better and some for the
" worse, the language of our Records was altered and turned into
" English. But at the Restoration of King Charles, this *novelty*
" was no longer countenanced; the practisers finding it very dif-
" ficult to express themselves so concisely or significantly in any
" other language but the Latin. And thus it continued without
" any sensible inconvenience till about the year 1730, when it was
" again thought proper that the proceedings at Law should be

If here *, as every where, he is eager to

" *done* into English, and it was accordingly so ordered by statute
" 4 Geo. II. c. 26.

" This was done (continues our Author) in order that the com-
" mon people might have knowledge and understanding of what
" was alleged or done for and against them in the process and
" pleadings, the judgment and entries in a cause. Which purpose
" I know not how well it has answered; but am *apt to suspect* that
" the people are now, after many years experience, *altogether* as
" ignorant in matters of law as before." .

In this scornful passage the words *novelty—done* into English—
apt to *suspect—altogether* as ignorant—sufficiently speak the affection of the mind that dictated it. It is thus that our Author
chuckles over the supposed defeat of the Legislature with a fond
exultation which all his discretion could not persuade him to
suppress.

The case is this. A large portion of the body of the Law was,
by the bigotry or the artifice of Lawyers, locked up in an illegible
character, and in a foreign tongue. The statute he mentions
obliged them to give up their hieroglyphicks, and to restore the
native language to its rights.

This was doing much; but it was not doing every thing. Fiction, tautology, technicality, circuity, irregularity, inconsistency
remain. But above all the pestilential breath of Fiction poisons
the sense of every instrument it comes near.

The consequence is, that the Law, and especially that part of it
which comes under the topic of Procedure, *still* wants much of
being generally intelligible. The fault then of the Legislature is
their not having done *enough.* His quarrel with them is for having done any thing at all. In doing what they did, they set up a
light, which, obscured by many remaining clouds, is still but too
apt to prove an *ignis fatuus*: our Author, instead of calling for

* V. infra, Ch. III. par. VII. p. 103.

hold the cup of flattery to high station, he

those clouds to be removed, deprecates all light, and pleads for total darkness.

Not content with representing the alteration as useless, he would persuade us to look upon it as mischievous. He speaks of " in-" conveniencies." What these inconveniencies are it is pleasant to observe.

In the first place, many young practisers, spoilt by the indul-gence of being permitted to carry on their business in their mother-tongue, know not how to read a Record upon the old plan. " Many Clerks and Attornies," says our Author, " are hardly able " to read, much less to understand a Record of so modern a date " as the reign of George the first."

What the mighty evil is here, that is to outweigh the mischief of almost universal ignorance, is not altogether clear: Whether it is, that certain Lawyers, in a case that happens very rarely, may be obliged to get assistance : or that the business in such a case may pass from those who do *not* understand it to those who do.

In the next place, he observes to us, " it has much enhanced " the expence of all legal proceedings : for since the practisers " are confined (for the sake of the stamp-duties, which are thereby " considerably encreased) to write only a stated number of words " in a sheet ; and as the English language, through the multitude " of its particles, is much more verbose than the Latin ; it follows, " that the number of sheets must be very much augmented by the " change."

I would fain persuade myself, were it possible, that this un-happy sophism could have passed upon the inventor. The sum actually levied on the public on that score is, upon the whole, either a proper sum or it is not. If it *is*, why mention it as an evil? If it is *not*, what more obvious remedy than to set the duties lower?

has stopt short, however, in this place, of ido-
latry [*t*].

After all, what seems to be the real evil, notwithstanding our Author's unwillingness to believe it, is, that by means of this alteration, men at large are in a somewhat better way of knowing what their Lawyers are about: and that a disinterested and enterprizing Legislator, should happily such an one arise, would now with somewhat less difficulty be able to see before him.

[*t*] In the Seventh Chapter of the First Book, the King has " *attributes* *," he possesses " *ubiquity†;*" he is " *all-perfect and* " *immortal‡* "

These childish paradoxes, begotten upon servility by false wit, are not more adverse to manly sentiment, than to accurate apprehension. Far from contributing to place the institutions they are applied to in any clear point of view, they serve but to dazzle and confound, by giving to Reality the air of Fable. It is true, they are not altogether of our Author's invention : it is he, however, that has revived them, and that with improvements and additions.

One might be apt to suppose they were no more than so many transient flashes of ornament : it is quite otherwise. He dwells upon them in sober sadness. The attribute of " *ubiquity,*" in particular, he lays hold of, and makes it the basis of a chain of reasoning. He spins it out into consequences: he makes one thing " *follow*" from it, and another thing be so and so " for the " same *reason :*" and he uses emphatic terms, as if for fear he should not be thought to be in earnest. " From the ubiquity," says our Author [1 Comm. p. 260.] " it *follows*, that the King " can never be nonsuit; *for* a nonsuit is the desertion of the suit or " action by the non-appearance of the plaintiff in Court."——

* 1 Comm. 242.

† 1 Comm. Ch. VII. p. 234, 238, 242, First Edition.

‡ 1 Comm. Ch. VII. p. 260, First Edition.

d

Reprehensible passages from the work at large.

It is not then, I say, *this* part, it is not even any part of that Introduction, to which alone I have any thoughts of extending my examination, that is the principal seat of that poison, against which it was the purpose of this attempt to give an antidote. The subject handled in this part of the work is such, as admits not of much to be said in the person of the Censor. Employed, as we have seen, in settling matters of a preliminary nature—in drawing outlines, it is not in this part that there was occasion to enter into the details of any particular institution. If 1 chose the Introduction then in preference to any other part, it was on account of its affording the fairest specimen of the whole, and not on account of its affording the greatest scope for censure.

" For the same reason also the King is not said to appear by his
" Attorney, as other men do ; for he always appears in contempla-
" tion of Law in his *own proper* person."

This is the case so soon as you come to this last sentence of the paragraph. For so long as you are at the last but two, " it is the " regal office, and *not* the royal person, that is always present." All this is so drily and so strictly true, that it serves as the groundwork of a metaphor that is brought in to embellish and enliven it. The King, we see, *is*, that is to say is *not*, present in Court. The King's Judges are present too. So far is plain downright truth. These Judges, then, speaking metaphorically, are so many looking-glasses, which have this singular property, that when a man looks at them, instead of seeing his own face in them, he sees the King's. " His Judges," says our Author, " are the mirror by which " the King's image is reflected."

Let us reverse the tablet. While with this freedom I expose our Author's ill deserts, let me not
be backward in acknowledging and paying homage
to his various merits: a justice due, not to him
alone, but to that Public, which now for so many
years has been dealing out to him (it cannot be
supposed altogether without title) so large a measure of its applause.

Correct, elegant, unembarrassed, ornamented,
the *style* is such, as could scarce fail to recommend
a work still more vitious in point of *matter* to the
multitude of readers.

He it is, in short, who, first of all institutional
writers, has taught Jurisprudence to speak the language of the Scholar and the Gentleman: put a
polish upon that rugged science: cleansed her
from the dust and cobwebs of the office : and if he
has not enriched her with that precision that is
drawn only from the sterling treasury of the
sciences, has decked her out, however, to advantage, from the toilette of classic erudition: en-
livened her with metaphors and allusions : and
sent her abroad in some measure to instruct, and
in still greater measure to entertain, the most mis-
cellaneous and even the most fastidious societies.

The merit to which, as much perhaps as to any,
the work stands indebted for its reputation, is the
enchanting harmony of its numbers: a kind of
merit that of itself is sufficient to give a certain

rita. degree of celebrity to a work devoid of every other. So much is man governed by the ear.

The function of the Expositor may be conceived to divide itself into two branches : that of *history,* and that of simple *demonstration.* The business of history is to represent the Law in the state it *has* been in, in past periods of its existence : the business of simple demonstration in the sense in which I will take leave to use the word, is to represent the Law in the state it *is* in for the time being [*v*].

Again, to the head of demonstration belong the several businesses of *arrangement, narration,* and *conjecture.* Matter of narration it may be called, where the Law is supposed to be explicit, clear, and settled : matter of conjecture or interpretation, where it is obscure, silent, or unsteady. It is matter of arrangement to *distribute* the several real or supposed institutions into different masses, for the purpose of a general survey ; to determine the *order* in which those masses shall be brought to view ; and to find for each of them a *name.*

[*v*] The word *demonstration* may here seem, at first sight, to be out of place. It will be easily perceived that the sense here put upon it is not the same with that in which it is employed by Logicians and Mathematicians. In our own language, indeed, it is not very familiar in any other sense than theirs : but on the Continent it is currently employed in many other sciences. The French, for example, have their *demonstrateurs de botanique, d'anatomie, de physique expérimantale, &c.* I use it out of necessity ; not knowing of any other that will suit the purpose.

The businesses of narration and interpretation are conversant chiefly about particular institutions. Into the details of particular institutions it has not been my purpose to descend. On these topics, then, I may say, in the language of procedure, *non sum informatus*. Viewing the work in this light, I have nothing to add to or to except against the public voice.

History is a branch of instruction which our Author, though not rigidly necessary to his design, called in, not without judgment, to cast light and ornament on the dull work of simple *demonstration:* this part he has executed with an elegance which strikes every one: with what fidelity, having not very particularly examined, I will not take upon me to pronounce.

Among the most difficult and the most important of the functions of the *demonstrator* is the business of *arrangement.* In this our Author has been thought, and not, I conceive, without justice, to excel; at least in comparison of any thing in that way that has hitherto appeared. 'Tis to him we owe such an arrangement of the elements of Jurisprudence, as wants little, perhaps, of being the best that a technical nomenclature will admit of. A technical nomenclature, so long as it is admitted to mark out and denominate the principal heads, stands an invincible obstacle to every other than a technical arrangement. For to *denominate* in

Its merits. general terms, what is it but to arrange? and to arrange under heads, what is it but to *denominate* upon a large scale? A technical arrangement, governed then in this manner, by a technical nomenclature, can never be otherwise than *confused* and *unsatisfactory*. The reason will be sufficiently apparent, when we understand what sort of an arrangement that must be which can be properly termed a *natural* one.

Idea of a natural arrangement. That arrangement of the materials of any science may, I take it, be termed a *natural* one, which takes such properties to characterize them by, as men in general are, by the common constitution of man's *nature*, disposed to attend to: such, in other words, as *naturally*, that is readily, engage, and firmly fix the attention of any one to whom they are pointed out. The materials, or elements here in question, are such actions as are the objects of what we call Laws or Institutions.

Now then, with respect to actions in general, there is no property in them that is calculated so readily to engage, and so firmly to fix the attention of an observer, as the *tendency* they may have *to*, or *divergency* (if one may so say) *from*, that which may be styled the common *end* of all of them. The end I mean is *Happiness* [w]: and this *tendency* in

[w] Let this be taken for a truth upon the authority of *Aristotle*: I mean by those, who like the authority of Aristotle better than that of their own experience. Πασα τεχνη, says that philosopher,

any act is what we style its *utility:* as this *diver-* Idea of a natural arrangement.
gency is that to which we give the name of *mis-*
chievousness. With respect then to such actions in
particular as are among the objects of the Law, to
point out to a man the *utility* of them or the mischievousness, is the only way to make him see
clearly that property of them which every man is
in search of; the only way, in short, to give him
satisfaction.

From *utility* then we may denominate a *principle,*
that may serve to preside over and govern, as it
were, such arrangement as shall be made of the
several institutions or combinations of institutions
that compose the matter of this science: and it is
this principle, that by putting its stamp upon the
several names given to those combinations, can
alone render *satisfactory* and *clear* any arrangement
that can be made of them.

Governed in this manner by a principle that is
recognized by all men, the same arrangement that
would serve for the jurisprudence of any one
country, would serve with little variation for that
of any other.

Yet more. The mischievousness of a bad Law
would be detected, at least the utility of it would be

καὶ πᾶσα μιθοδος· ὁμοίως δι πρᾶξίς τι καὶ προαιρισις, ἀγαθου τινος
ἐφιισθαι δοκιι· διο καλως ἀπιφηναντο ταγαθον, ου παντα ἐφιται.
Διαφορα δι τις φαινιται των (understand τουτων ΤΕΛΩΝ.—Arist.
Eth. ad Nic. L. I. c. 1.

rendered suspicious, by the difficulty of finding a place for it in such an arrangement : while, on the other hand, a *technical* arrangement is a sink that with equal facility will swallow any garbage that is thrown into it.

That this advantage may be possessed by a natural arrangement, is not difficult to conceive. Institutions would be characterized by it in the only universal way in which they can be characterized ; by the nature of the several *modes* of *conduct* which, by prohibiting, they constitute *offences* [x].

These offences would be collected into classes denominated by the various modes of their *divergency* from the common *end*; that is, as we have said, by their various forms and degrees of *mischievousness :* in a word, by those properties which are *reasons* for their being made *offences :* and whether any such mode of conduct possesses any such property is a question of experience [y]. Now, a bad Law is that which prohibits a mode of conduct that is *not* mischievous [z]. Thus would it be found impracticable to place the mode of conduct prohibited by a bad law under any denomination of

[x] Offences, the reader will remember, may as well be offences of *omission*, as of *commission*. I would avoid the embarrassment of making separate mention of such Laws as exert themselves in *commanding*. 'Tis on this account I use the phrase " *mode of* " *conduct*," which includes *omissions* or *forbearances*, as well as *acts*.

[y] See note [ee].   [z] See note [x].

offence, without asserting such a matter of fact as Idea of a
natural ar-
rangement. is contradicted by experience. Thus cultivated, in short, the soil of Jurisprudence would be found to repel in a manner every evil institution; like that country which refuses, we are told, to harbour any thing venomous in its bosom.

The *synopsis* of such an arrangement would at once be a compendium of *expository* and of *censorial* Jurisprudence: nor would it serve more effectually to instruct the *subject*, than it would to justify or reprove the *Legislator*.

Such a synopsis, in short, would be at once a map, and that an universal one, of Jurisprudence as it *is*, and a slight but comprehensive sketch of what it *ought to be*. For, the *reasons* of the several institutions comprized under it would stand expressed, we see, and that uniformly (as in our Author's synopsis they do in scattered instances) by the names given to the several classes under which those institutions are comprized. And what reasons? Not *technical* reasons, such as none but a Lawyer gives, nor any but a Lawyer would put up with [aa]; but reasons, such as were they in

---

[aa] *Technical* reasons: so called from the the Greek τέχνη, which signifies an art, science, or profession.

Utility is that standard to which men in general, (except in here and there an instance where they are deterred by prejudices of the religious class, or hurried away by the force of what is called *sentiment* or *feeling*). Utility, as we have said, is the

themselves what they might and ought to be, and
expressed too in the manner they might and ought
to be, any man might see the force of as well as he.

Nor in this is there any thing that need surprize
us. The consequences of any Law, or of any act
which is made the object of a Law, the only consequences that men are at all interested in, what are
they but *pain* and *pleasure?* By some such words
then as *pain* and *pleasure*, they may be expressed:
and *pain* and *pleasure* at least, are words which a
man has no need, we may hope, to go to a Lawyer
to know the meaning of [*bb*]. In the synopsis then
of that sort of arrangement which alone deserves
the name of a natural one, terms such as these,
terms which if they can be said to belong to any
science, belong rather to Ethics than to Jurispru-

standard to which they refer a Law or institution in judging of its
title to approbation or disapprobation. Men of Law, corrupted
by interests, or seduced by illusions, which it is not here our
business to display, have deviated from it much more frequently,
and with much less reserve. Hence it is that such reasons as
pass with Lawyers, and with no one else, have got the name of
technical reasons; reasons peculiar to the *art*, peculiar to the
profession.

[*bb*] The *reason* of a Law, in short, is no other than the *good*
produced by the mode of conduct which it enjoins, or (which
comes to the same thing) the *mischief* produced by the mode of
conduct which it prohibits. This *mischief* or this *good*, if they be
real, cannot but shew themselves somewhere or other in the shape
of *pain* or *pleasure*.

dence, even than to universal Jurisprudence, will Idea of a
natural ar-
rangement. engross the most commanding stations.

What then is to be done with those names of classes that are purely technical?—With offences, for example, against prerogative, with misprisions, contempts, felonies, præmunires [cc]? What relation is it that these mark out between the Laws that concern the sorts of acts they are respectively put to signify, and that *common end* we have been speaking of? Not any. In a natural arrangement what then would become of them? They would either be banished at once to the region of *quiddities* and *substantial forms;* or if, and in deference to attachments too inveterate to be all at once dissolved, they were still to be indulged a place, they would be stationed in the corners and bye-places of the Synopsis: stationed, not as now to *give* light, but to *receive* it. But more of this, perhaps, at some future time.

To return to our Author. Embarrassed, as a man must needs be, by this blind and intractable nomenclature, he will be found, I conceive, to have done as much as could reasonably be expected of a writer so circumstanced; and more and better than was ever done before by any one.

In one part, particularly, of his Synopsis *, se- Merits of
the work
resumed.

[cc] See in the Synoptical Table prefixed to our Author's *Analysis,* the last page comprehending Book IV.

* It is that which comprizes his IVth Book, intitled PUBLIC

veral fragments of a sort of method which is, or at
least comes near to, what may be termed a natural
one [*dd*], are actually to be found.   We there read
of " *corporal injuries* ;" of " offences against *peace* ;"
against " *health* ;" against " *personal security* [*ee*] ;"
" *liberty* :"—" *property* :"——light is let in, though
irregularly, at various places.

In an unequal imitation of this Synopsis that has
lately been performed upon what is called the *Civil
Law, all* is technical.   All in short, is darkness.
Scarce a syllable by which a man would be led to
suspect, that the affair in hand were an affair that

[*dd*] *Fragmenta methodi naturalis.*—Linnæi *Phil. Bot.* Tit.
Systemata, par. 77.

[*ee*] This title affords a pertinent instance to exemplify the use
that a natural arrangement may be of in repelling an incompetent
institution.   What I mean is the sort of filthiness that is termed
unnatural. This our Author has ranked in his class of *Offences
against* " *personal security,*" and, in a subdivision of it, intitled
" *Corporal Injuries.*" In so doing, then, he has asserted a fact :
he has asserted that the offence in question is an offence against
personal security ; is a corporal injury ; is, in short, productive of
unhappiness *in that way.* Now this is what, in the case where
the act is committed *by consent,* is manifestly not true.   *Volenti
non fit injuria.* If then the Law against the offence in question
had no other title to a place in the system than what was founded
on this *fact,* it is plain it would have none.   It would be a bad
Law altogether.   The mischief the offence is of to the community
in this case is in truth of quite another nature, and would come
under quite another class.   When *against* consent, there indeed
it does belong really to this class : but then it would come under
another name.   It would come under that of *Rape.*

happiness or unhappiness was at all concerned
in [*ff*].

To return, once more, to our Author's Commentaries. Not even in a *censorial* view would I be understood to deem them altogether without merit. For the institutions commented on, where they are capable of good reasons, good reasons are every now and then given: in which way, so far as it goes, one-half of the Censor's talk is well accomplished. Nor is the dark side of the picture left absolutely untouched. Under the head of " Trial " by Jury," are some very just and interesting remarks on the yet-remaining imperfections of that

[*ff*] I think it is Selden, somewhere in his *Table-talk*, that speaks of a whimsical notion he had hit upon when a school boy, that with regard to *Cæsar* and *Justin*, and those other personages of antiquity that gave him so much trouble, there was not a syllable of truth in any thing they said, nor in fact were there ever really any such persons; but that the whole affair was a contrivance of parents to find employment for their children. Much the same sort of notion is that which these technical arrangements are calculated to give us of Jurisprudence : which in them stands represented rather as a game at *Crambo* for Lawyers to whet their wits at, than as that Science which holds in her hand the happiness of nations.

Let us, however, do no man wrong. Where the success has been worse, the difficulty was greater. That detestable chaos of institutions which the Analyst last-mentioned had to do with, is still more embarrassed with a technical nomenclature than our own.

Merits of
the work
resumed.

mode of trial*: and under that of " Assurances
" by matter of Record," on the lying and extor-
tious jargon of *Recoveries* †.   So little, however,
are these particular remarks of a piece with the
general disposition, that shews itself so strongly
throughout the work, indeed so plainly adverse to
the general maxims that we have seen, that I can
scarce bring myself to attribute them to our Author.
Not only disorder is announced by them, but remedies, well-imagined remedies, are pointed out.
One would think some Angel had been sowing
wheat among our Author's tares [gg].

Manner in
which the
present Essay
has been con-
ducted.

With regard to this Essay itself, I have not much
to say.   The principal and professed purpose of it

* 3 Comm. Ch. XXIII. p. 387.

† 2 Comm. Ch. XXI. p. 360.

[gg] The difference between a generous and determined affection, and an occasional, and as it were forced contribution, to the
cause of reformation, may be seen, I think, in these Commentaries,
compared with another celebrated work on the subject of our
Jurisprudence.   Mr. Barrington, whose agreeable Miscellany has
done so much towards opening men's eyes upon this subject; Mr.
Barrington, like an active General in the service of the Public,
storms the strong-holds of chicane, wheresoever they present
themselves, and particularly fictions, without reserve.   Our Author, like an artful partizan in the service of the profession, sacri-
fices a few, as if it were to save the rest.

Deplorable, indeed, would have been the student's chance for
salutary instruction, did not Mr. Barrington's work in so many
instances, furnish the antidote to our Author's poisons.

is, to expose the errors and insufficiencies of our Author. The business of it is therefore rather to overthrow than to *set up;* which latter task can seldom be performed to any great advantage where the former is the principal one.

To guard against the danger of misrepresentation, and to make sure of doing our Author no injustice, his own words are given all along: and, as scarce any sentence is left unnoticed, the whole comment wears the form of what is called a perpetual one. With regard to a discourse that is simply institutional, and in which the writer builds upon a plan of his own, a great part of the satisfaction it can be made to afford depends upon the order and connection that are established between the several parts of it. In a comment upon the work of another, no such connection, or at least no such order, can be established commodiously, if at all. The order of the comment is prescribed by the order, perhaps the disorder, of the text.

The chief employment of this Essay, as we have said, has necessarily been *to overthrow.* In the little, therefore, which has been done by it in the way of *setting up,* my view has been not so much to think for the Reader, as to put him upon thinking for himself. This I flatter myself with having done on several interesting topics; and this is all that at present I propose.

Among the few positions of my own which I

Manner in
which the
present Essay
has been con-
ducted.
have found occasion to advance, some I observe
which promise to be far from popular. These it is
likely may give rise to very warm objections : objections which in themselves I do not wonder at,
and which in their motive I cannot but approve.
The people are a set of masters whom it is not in a
man's power in every instance fully to please, and
at the same time faithfully to serve.   He that is re-
solved to persevere without deviation in the line of
truth and utility, must have learnt to prefer the still
whisper of enduring approbation, to the short-lived
bustle of tumultuous applause.

Other passages too there may be, of which some
farther explanation may perhaps not unreasonably
be demanded.   But to give these explanations, and
to obviate those objections, is a task which, if executed at all, must be referred to some other opportunity.   Consistency forbad our expatiating so far
as to lose sight of our Author : since it was the line
of his course that marked the boundaries of ours.

A

FRAGMENT

ON

GOVERNMENT.

─────

INTRODUCTION.

I. THE subject of this examination, is a passage INTRODUC-
contained in that part of Sir W. BLACKSTONE's TION.
COMMENTARIES on the LAWS of ENGLAND, which Division of
the Author has stiled the INTRODUCTION. This our Author's Introduction.
Introduction of his stands divided into four Sec-
tions. The *first* contains his discourse " *On the*
" STUDY *of the* LAW." The *second*, entitled " *Of the*
" NATURE *of* LAWS *in general,*" contains his speculations concerning the various objects, real or
imaginary, that are in use to be mentioned under
the common name of LAW. The *third*, entitled
" *Of the* LAWS *of* ENGLAND," contains such general
observations, relative to these last mentioned Laws,
as seemed proper to be premised before he entered

B

INTRODUC-
TION.

into the details of any parts of them in particular. In the *fourth*, entitled, *Of the* COUNTRIES *subject to the "* LAWS *of* ENGLAND," is given a statement of the different territorial extents of different branches of those Laws.

What part of
it is here to
be examined.

II. 'Tis in the *second* of these Sections, that we shall find the passage proposed for examination. It occupies in the edition I happen to have before me, (1768) which is the *first* (and all the editions, I believe, are paged alike) the space of *seven* pages ; from the 47th, to the 53d, inclusive.

His definition
of Law Muni-
cipal.

III. After treating of " LAW *in general,*" of the " LAW of *Nature,*" " LAW of *Revelation,*" and " LAW " of *Nations,*" branches of that imaginary whole, our Author comes at length to what he calls " LAW " *municipal :*" that sort of Law, to which men in their ordinary discourse would give the name of Law without addition ; the only sort perhaps of them all (unless it be that of *Revelation*) to which the name can, with strict propriety, be applied : in a word, that sort which we see made in each nation, to express the will of that body in it which governs. On this subject of LAW *Municipal* he sets out, as a man ought, with a *definition* of the phrase itself; an important and fundamental phrase, which stood highly in need of a definition, and never so much as since our Author has defined it.

IV. This definition is ushered in with no small
[...]play of accuracy. First, it is given entire : it is
[...]en taken to pieces, clause by clause; and every A digression
in the middle
of it. Its ge-
neral con-
tents.
[...]use, by itself, justified and explained. In
[...] very midst of these explanations, in the
[...]ry midst of the definition, he makes a sudden
[...]nd. And now it bethinks him that it is a good
[...]e to give a dissertation, or rather a bundle of
[...]ssertations, upon various subjects—On the *man-
[...]r* in which *Governments were* established—On the
[...]ferent *forms* they assume when they *are* estab-
[...]hed—On the peculiar excellence of that form
[...]ich is established in *this country*—On the *right*,
[...]ich he thinks it necessary to tell us, the GOVERN-
[...]NT in every country has, of making LAWS—On
[...] *duty* of making LAWS ; which, he says, is also
[...]umbent on the Government.—In stating these
[...]o last heads, I give, as near as possible, his own
[...]*rds ;* thinking it premature to engage in discus-
[...]ns, and not daring to decide without discussion,
[...]the *sense*.

V. The digression we are about to examine, is, This digression the sub-
ject of the
present exa-
mination.
[...]it happens, not at all involved with the body of
[...] work from which it starts. No mutual refe-
[...]ces or allusions: no supports or illustrations
[...]mmunicated or received. It may be considered as
[...]e small work inserted into a large one; the con-
[...]*ning* and the contain*ed*, having scarce any other

connection than what the operations of the press
have given them. It is this disconnection that will
enable us the better to bestow on the latter a separate
examination, without breaking in upon any thread
of reasoning, or any principle of order.

VI. A general statement of the topics touched
upon in the digression we are about to examine,
has been given above. It will be found, I trust, a
faithful one. It will not be thought, however, much
of a piece, perhaps, with the following, which our
Author himself has given us. " This," (says he *,
meaning an explanation he had been giving of a part
of the definition above spoken of) " will naturally
" lead us into a short enquiry into the nature
" of society and civil government [a] ; and the na-

---

* 1 Comm. p. 47.

[a] To make sure of doing our Author no injustice, and to shew
what it is that he thought would " naturally lead us into " this
" enquiry," it may be proper to give the paragraph containing the
explanation above mentioned. It is as follows :—" But farther :
" municipal Law is a rule of civil conduct, prescribed by the supreme
" power in a state." " For Legislature, as was before observed, is
" the greatest act of superiority that can be exercised by one being
" over another. Wherefore it is requisite, to the very essence of a
" Law, that it be made" (he might have added, " or at least sup-
" ported ") by the supreme power. Sovereignty and Legislature
" are indeed convertible terms; one cannot subsist without the
" other." 1 Comm. p. 46.

tural inherent right that belongs to the sovereignty of a state, wherever that sovereignty be
lodged, of making and enforcing Laws."

VII. No very explicit mention here, we may
serve, of the *manner* in which Governments have
en established, or of the different *forms* they as-
me when established; no very explicit intimation
at these were among the topics to be discussed.
one at all of the *duty* of Government to make
ws: none at all of the *British constitution;*
ough, of the four other topics we have mentioned,
ere is no one on which he has been near so copi-
s as on this last. The *right* of Government to
ake Laws, that delicate and invidious topic, as we
all find it when explained, is that which, for the
oment, seems to have swallowed up almost the
ole of his attention.

VIII. Be this as it may, the contents of the dis-
rtation before us, taken as I have stated them,
ll furnish us with the matter of five chapters:—
e, which I shall entitle " FORMATION *of* Go-
VERNMENT "—a second, " FORMS *of* GOVERN-
MENT "—a third, " BRITISH CONSTITUTION "—
fourth, " RIGHT *of the* SUPREME POWER *to make*
LAWS "—a fifth " DUTY *of the* SUPREME POWER
to make LAWS."

CHAP. I.

FORMATION OF GOVERNMENT.

CHAP. I.

Subject of the passage to be examined in the present chapter.

I. THE first object which our Author seems to have proposed to himself in the dissertation we are about to examine, is to give us an idea of the *manner* in which Governments were formed. This occupies the first paragraph, together with part of the second: for the *typographical* division does not seem to quadrate very exactly with the *intellectual*. As the examination of this passage will unavoidably turn in great measure upon the words, it will be proper the reader should have it under his eye.

The passage recited.

II. " The only true and natural foundations of " *society*," (says our Author*) " are the wants and " the fears of individuals. Not that we can believe, " with some theoretical writers, that there ever was " a time when there was no such thing as *society* ; " and that, from the impulse of reason, and through " a sense of their wants and weaknesses, indivi- " duals met together in a large plain, entered into " an *original contract,* and chose the tallest man

---

* 1 Comm. p. 47.

" present to be their governor. This notion, of an CHAP. I.
" actually existing unconnected *state of nature*, is
" too wild to be seriously admitted; and besides,
" it is plainly contradictory to the revealed accounts
" of the primitive origin of mankind, and their pre-
" servation two thousand years afterwards; both
" which were effected by the means of single
" families. These formed the first *society*, among
" themselves; which every day extended its limits,
" and when it grew too large to subsist with conveni-
" ence in that pastoral state, wherein the Patriarchs
" appear to have lived, it necessarily subdivided
" itself by various migrations into more. After-
" wards, as agriculture increased, which employs
" and can maintain a much greater number of
" hands, migrations became less frequent; and
" various tribes, which had formerly separated, re-
" united again; sometimes by compulsion and con-
" quest, sometimes by accident, and sometimes
" perhaps by compact. But though *Society* had
" not its formal beginning from any convention of
" individuals, actuated by their wants and their
" fears; yet it is the *sense* of their weakness and
" imperfection that *keeps* mankind together; that
" demonstrates the necessity of this union; and
" that therefore is the solid and natural foundation,
" as well as the cement, of *society*: And this is
" what we mean by the *original contract* of *society*:
" which, though perhaps in no instance it has ever

CHAP. I. "been formally expressed at the first institution of
"a state, yet in nature and reason must always be
"understood and implied, in the very act of asso-
"ciating together: namely, that the whole should
"protect all its parts, and that every part should pay
"obedience to the will of the whole; or, in other
"words, that the community should guard the
"rights of each individual member, and that (in re-
"turn for this protection) each individual should
"submit to the laws of the community; without
"which submission of all it was impossible that
"protection could be certainly extended to any.

"For when *society* is once formed, *government*
"results of course, as necessary to preserve and to
"keep that *society* in order. Unless some superior
"were constituted, whose commands and decisions
"all the members are bound to obey, they would
"still remain as in a *state of nature*, without any
"judge upon earth to define their several rights,
"and redress their several wrongs."—Thus far our
Author.

Confusion among the leading terms of it. III. When leading terms are made to chop and
change their several significations; sometimes
meaning one thing, sometimes another, at the up-
shot perhaps nothing; and this in the compass of a
paragraph; one may judge what will be the complection of the whole context. This, we shall see,
is the case with the chief of those we have been

reading : for instance, with the words " Society,"—
" state of nature,"—" original contract,"— not to
tire the reader with any more. " *Society*," in one
place means the same thing as " *a state of nature*"
does : in another place it means the same as " *Government.*" Here, we are required to believe there *never
was* such a state as a state of nature : there, we are
given to understand there *has been*. In like manner
with respect to an *original contract* we are given to
understand that such a thing never existed ; that
the notion of it is even ridiculous : at the same time
that there is no speaking nor stirring without supposing that there was one.

IV. First, Society means a *state of nature*. For
if by " *a state of nature*" a man means any thing, it
is the state, I take it, men are in or supposed to be
in, before they are under *government* : the state men
quit when they enter into a state of government ;
and in which, were it not for government, they
would remain. But by the word " *society*" it is plain
at one time that he means that state. First, according
to him, comes *society* ; then afterwards comes *government*. " For when society," says our Author, " is
" once formed, government results of course ; as
" necessary to preserve and keep that society in
" order *."—And again, immediately afterwards,—
" A state in which a superior has been constituted,

Margin note: "Society" not synonymous to a state of nature.—opposed to "Government."—and spoken of as having existed.

* v. supra p. 11.

CHAP I.   " whose commands and decisions all the members " are bound to obey," he puts as an explanation (nor is it an inapt one) of a state of " *government :*" and " unless" men were in a state of that description, they would still " remain," he says, " as in " a *state of nature.*" By *society*, therefore, he means, once more, the same as by a " *state of nature :*" he *opposes* it to *government.* And he speaks of it as a state which, in this sense, has actually existed.

"Society" put synonymous to " government."

V. Secondly, This is what he tells us in the beginning of the *second* of the two paragraphs : but all the time the *first* paragraph lasted, *society* meant the same as *government.* In shifting then from one paragraph to another, it has changed its nature. 'Tis " the foundations of *society**,*" that he first began to speak of; and immediately he goes on to explain to us, after his manner of explaining, the foundations of *government.* 'Tis of a " formal be-" ginning" of " Society †," that he speaks soon after; and by this formal beginning, he tells us *immediately, that he means, " the *original contract* of " *society ‡,*" which contract entered into " a *state* §," he gives us to understand, is thereby " instituted," and men have undertaken to " submit to Laws ‖."

---

* 1 Comm. p. 47. supra p. 6.   † 1 Comm. p. 47. supra p. 7.
‡ 1 Comm. p. 47. supra p. 7.   § 1 Comm. p. 47. supra p. 8.
‖ 1 Comm. p. 48. supra p. 8.

So long then as this first paragraph lasts, " *society*," CHAP. I.
I think, it is plain cannot but have been meaning the
same as " *government*."

VI. Thirdly, All this while too, this same " *state* A state of nature spoken of, as never having existed.
" *of nature*" to which we have seen " *Society*" (a
state spoken of as existing) put synonymous, and in
which were it not for *government*, men, he informs
us, in the next page, would " *remain**," is a state in
which they never *were*. So he expressly tells us.
This " notion," says he, " of an actually existing un-
" connected state of nature ;" (that is, as he explains himself afterwards † " a state in which men
" have no judge to define their rights, and redress
" their wrongs,) is too wild to be seriously ad-
" mitted ‡." When he admits it then himself, as he
does in his next page, we are to understand, it
seems, that he is bantering us : and that the next
paragraph is (what one should not otherwise have
taken it for) a piece of pleasantry.

VII. Fourthly, The *original contract* is a thing, *Original contract,* its reality denied--
we are to understand, that never had existence;
perhaps not in *any* state : certainly therefore not in
all. " Perhaps, in no instance," says our Author,

---

* 1 Comm. p. 48. supra p. 8.   † 1 Comm. p. 48. supra p. 8.

‡ 1 Comm. p. 47. supra p. 7.

CHAP. I.   " has it ever been formally expressed at the first in-
            " stitution of a state *."

---asserted.   VIII. Fifthly, Notwithstanding all this, we must
            suppose, it seems, that it had in *every* state: " yet
            " in nature and reason," (says our Author) " it must
            " always be understood and implied †." Growing
            bolder in the compass of four or five pages, where
            he is speaking of our own Government, he asserts
            roundly ‡, that such a contract was actually made at
            the first formation of it. " The legislature would be
            " changed," he says, " from that which *was origi-*
            " *nally* set up by the general consent and funda-
            " mental act of the society."

Attempt to   IX. Let us try whether it be not possible for
reconcile
these contra- something to be done towards drawing the import
dictions—
Society   of these terms out of the mist in which our Author
distinguished
into natural   has involved them. The word " SOCIETY," I think,
and political.
            it appears, is used by him, and that without notice,
            in two senses that are opposite. In the one, so-
            CIETY, or a STATE of SOCIETY, is put *synonymous*
            to a STATE of NATURE; and stands *opposed* to
            GOVERNMENT, or a STATE OF GOVERNMENT: in.
            this sense it may be styled, as it commonly is, *na-*
            tural SOCIETY. In the other, it is put *synonymous* to

            * 1 Comm. p. 46. supra p. 7,   † 1 Comm. p. 46. supra p. 7.
                        ‡ 1 Comm. p. 52.

GOVERNMENT, or a STATE OF GOVERNMENT; and CHAP. I.
stands *opposed* to a STATE OF NATURE: in this sense
it may be styled, as it commonly is, *political* society. Of the difference between these two states,
a tolerably distinct idea, I take it, may be given in
a word or two.

X. The idea of a natural society is a *negative* one. Idea of
The idea of a political society is a *positive* one. political
society.
'Tis with the latter, therefore, we should begin.

When a number of persons (whom we may style
subjects) are supposed to be in the *habit* of paying
obedience to a person, or an assemblage of persons,
of a known and certain description (whom we may
call *governor* or *governors*) such persons altogether
(*subjects* and *governors*) are said to be in a state of
political SOCIETY *.

XI. The idea of a state of *natural* SOCIETY is, as Idea of
natural
we have said, a *negative* one. When a number of society.
persons are supposed to be in the habit of *conversing*
with each other, at the same time that they are not in
any such habit as mentioned above, they are said to
be in a state of *natural* SOCIETY.

XII. If we reflect a little, we shall perceive, that, Difficulty of
drawing
between these two states, there is not that explicit the line between the
separation which these names, and these definitions, two states.

* v. infra. par. 12. note [*b*.]

CHAP. I. might teach one, at first sight, to expect. It is with
them as with light and darkness : however distinct
the ideas may be, that are, at first mention, suggested by those *names*, the *things* themselves have
no determinate bound to separate them.   The circumstance that has been spoken of as constituting
the difference between these two states, is the presence or absence of an *habit of obedience*. This habit,
accordingly, has been spoken of simply as *present*
(that is as being *perfectly* present) or, in other words,
we have spoken as if there were a *perfect* habit of
obedience, in the *one* case : it has been spoken of
simply as *absent* (that is as being *perfectly* absent)
or, in other words, we have spoken as if there were
no habit of obedience at all, in the *other*. But neither of these manners of speaking, perhaps, is
strictly just.   Few, in fact, if any, are the instances
of this habit being perfectly *absent ;* certainly none
at all, of its being perfectly *present*.   Governments
accordingly, in proportion as the habit of obedience
is more perfect, recede from, in proportion as it is
less perfect, approach to, a state of nature : and instances may present themselves in which it shall be
difficult to say whether a habit, perfect, in the degree in which, to constitute a government, it is
deemed necessary it *should* be perfect, *does* subsist
or *not* [b].

A habit.   [b] 1. A *habit* is but an assemblage of *acts* : under which name I
would also include, for the present, *voluntary forbearances.*

XIII. On these considerations, the supposition of a *perfect state of nature*, or, as it may be termed, a state of *society perfectly natural*, may, perhaps, be justly pronounced what our Author for the moment

CHAP. I.
A perfect state of nature not more chimerical than a perfect state of government.

2. A *habit of obedience* then is an assemblage of *acts of obedience*.

A habit of obedience.

3. An *act of obedience* is any act done in pursuance of an *expression of will* on the part of some *superior*.

An act of obedience.

4. An *act of* POLITICAL *obedience* (which is what is here meant) is any act done in pursuance of an expression of will on the part of a person governing.

An act of political obedience.

5. An *expression of will* is either *parole* or *tacit*.

An expression of will.

6. A *parole expression of will* is that which is conveyed by the signs called *words*.

A parole expression of will.

7. A *tacit expression of will* is that which is conveyed by any other *signs* whatsoever: among which none are so efficacious as *acts* of *punishment*, annexed in time past, to the non performance of acts of the same sort with those that are the objects of the will that is in question.

A tacit expression of will.

8. A *parole* expression of the will of a superior is a *command*.

A command.

9. When a *tacit* expression of the will of a superior is supposed to have been uttered, it may be styled a *fictitious command*.

A *fictitious* command.

10. Were we at liberty to coin words after the manner of the Roman lawyers, we might say a *quasi*-command.

Commands ✕ quasi-commands.

11. The STATUTE LAW is composed of *commands*. The COMMON LAW, of *quasi*-commands.

Illustration—Statute Law, ✕ Common Law.

12. An act which is the object of a command actual or fictitious; such an act, considered before it is performed, is styled a *duty*, or a *point of duty*.

Duty—point of duty.

13. These definitions premised, we are now in a condition to give such an idea, of what is meant by the *perfection* or *imperfection* of a *habit of obedience* in a society as may prove tolerably precise.

Use of the above chain of definitions.

CHAP. I. seemed to think it, an extravagant supposition : but then that of a *government* in this sense *perfect* ; or, as it may be termed, a state of society *perfectly politi-*

Habit of obedience—measure of its perfection.

14. A *period* in the duration of the society ; the number of *persons* it is composed of during that period ; and the number of *points of duty* incumbent on each person being given ;—the habit of obedience will be more or less *perfect*, in the ratio of the number of acts of *obedience* to those of *disobedience*.

Illustration.

15. The habit of obedience in this country appears to have been more perfect in the time of the Saxons than in that of the Britons : unquestionably it is more so now than in the time of the Saxons. It is not yet so perfect, as well contrived and well digested laws in time, it is to be hoped, may render it. But absolutely perfect, till man ceases to be man, it never *can* be.

A very ingenious and instructive view of the progress of nations, from the least perfect states of political union to that highly perfect state of it in which we live, may be found in LORD KAIMS's *Historical Law Tracts.*

Political union or connection.

16. For the convenience and accuracy of discourse it may be of use, in this place, to settle the signification of a few other expressions relative to the same subject. Persons who, with respect to each other, are in a state of *political society*, may be said also to be in a state of *political union* or *connection*.

Submission—subjection.

17. Such of them as are *subjects* may, accordingly, be said to be in a state of *submission*, or of *subjection*, with respect to *governors* : such as are *governors* in a state of *authority* with respect to *subjects.*

Submission)(subjection.

18. When the subordination is considered as resulting originally from the *will*, or (it may be more proper to say) the *pleasure* of the party governed, we rather use the word "*submission*:" when from that of the party governing, the word "*subjection*." On this account it is that the term can scarcely be used without apology, unless with a note of disapprobation : especially in this country,

, a state of *perfect political union*, a state of *per-*
t *submission* in the *subject*, of *perfect authority* in
: *governor*, is no less so[c].

:re the habit of considering the *consent* of the persons governed
)eing in some sense or other involved in the notion of all *law-*
. that is, all *commendable* government, has gained so firm a
ond. It is on this account, then, that the term " *subjection*,"
luding as it does, or, at least, not including such consent, is used
imonly in what is called a BAD sense : that is, in such a sense
together with the idea of the object in question, conveys the
essary idea of disapprobation. This accessary idea, however,
exed as it is to the *abstract* term " subjection," does not extend
lf to the *concrete* term " subjects"—a kind of inconsistency of
ich there are many instances in language.

c] It is true that every person must, for some time, at least, after *It is not a*
birth, necessarily be in a state of subjection with respect to his *family union,*
                                                                      however per-
ents, or those who stand in the place of parents to him ; and *fect, that can*
                                                               constitute
t a perfect one, or at least as near to being a perfect one, as any *a political so-*
                                                                     ciety—why.
t we see. But for all this, the sort of society that is constituted
a state of subjection thus circumstanced, does not come up to
idea that, I believe, is generally entertained by those who
:ak of a *political* society. To constitute what is meant in gene-
by that phrase, a greater *number* of members is required, or,
least, a *duration* capable of a longer continuance. Indeed, for
i purpose nothing 'less, I take it, than an *indefinite* duration is
juired. A society, to come within the notion of what is ordi-
ily meant by a *political* one, must be such as, in its nature, is
: incapable of continuing for ever in virtue of the principles
ich gave it birth. This, it is plain, is not the case with such a
nily society, of which a parent, or a pair of parents are at the
id. In such a society, the only principle of union which is cer-
n and uniform in its operation, is the natural weakness of those
its members that are in a state of subjection; that is, the chil-

CHAP. I.

" State of na-
" ture" a re-
lative expres-
sion.

XIV. A remark there is, which, for the more thoroughly clearing up of our notions on this subject, it may be proper here to make. To some ears, the phrases, " state of nature," " state of political so- " ciety," may carry the appearance of being *absolute* in their signification :. as if the condition of a man, or a company of men, in one of these states, or in the other, where a matter that depended altogether upon themselves. But this is not the case. To the expression " state of nature," no more than to the expression " state of political society," can any pre- cise meaning be annexed, without reference to a party different from that one who is spoken of as being in the state in question. This will readily be perceived. The difference between the two states

---

dren : a principle which has but a short and limited continuance. I question whether it be the case even with a family society, sub- sisting in virtue of *collateral* consanguinity ; and that for the like reason. Not but that even in this case a habit of obedience, as perfect as any we see examples of, may subsist for a time; to wit, in virtue of the same *moral* principles which may protract a habit, of *filial* obedience beyond the continuance of the *physical* ones which gave birth to it : I mean affection, gratitude, awe, the force of habit, and the like. But it is not long, even in this case, before the bond of connection must either become imperceptible, or lose its influence by being too extended.

These considerations, therefore, it will be proper to bear in mind in applying the definition of political society above given [in par. 10.] and in order to reconcile it with what is said further on [in par. 17.].

lies, as we have observed, in the *habit of obedience.* With respect then to a habit of obedience, it can neither be understood as subsisting, in any person, nor as not subsisting, but with reference to some other person. For one party to *obey,* there must be another party that is obeyed. But this party who is obeyed, may at different times be different. Hence may one and the same party be conceived to obey and *not* to obey at the same time, so as it be with respect to different *persons,* or, as we may say, to different *objects of obedience.* Hence it is, then, that one and the same party may be said to *be* in a state of nature and *not* to be in a state of nature, and that at one and the same time, according as it is this or *that* party that is taken for the other object of comparison. The case is, that in common speech, when no particular object of comparison is specified, all persons in general are intended: so that when a number of persons are said simply to be in a state of nature, what is understood is, that they are so as well with reference to one another, as to all the world.

XV. In the same manner we may understand, how the same man, who is *governor* with respect to one man or set of men, may be *subject* with respect to another: how among governors some may be in a *perfect* state of *nature* with respect to each other: as the KINGS of FRANCE and SPAIN: others, again,

CHAP. I. in a state of *perfect subjection*, as the HOSPODARS of WALACHIA and MOLDAVIA with respect to the GRAND SIGNIOR:. others, again, in a state of. manifest but *imperfect subjection*, as the GERMAN. States with respect to the EMPEROR.: others, again, . in such a state in which it may be difficult to determine whether they are in a state of *imperfect sub-.jection* or in a *perfect* state of *nature :* as the KING. of NAPLES with respect to the POPE [*d*].

The same person alternately in a state of political and natural society with respect to different societies.

XVI. In the same manner, also, it may be conceived, without entering into details, how any single person, born, as all persons are born, into a perfect subjection to his parents*, that is into a state of perfect political society with respect to his parents, may from thence pass into a perfect state of nature ; and from thence successively into any number of different states of political society more or less perfect, by passing into different societies.

In the same political society the same persons alternately, governors and subjects, with respect to the same persons.

XVII. In the same manner also it may be conceived how, in any political society, the same man

[*d*] The Kingdom of Naples is feudatory to the Papal See: and in token of fealty, the King, at his accession, presents the Holy Father with a white horse. The royal vassal sometimes treats his Lord but cavalierly : but always sends him his white horse.

* V. supra, par. 13. note [*c*].

may, with respect to the same individuals, be, at
different periods, and on different occasions, alternately, in the state of governor and subject: to-day
concurring, perhaps active, in the business of issuing a *general* command for the observance of the
whole society, amongst the rest of another man in
quality of *Judge:* to-morrow, punished, perhaps, by
a *particular* command of that same Judge for not
obeying the general command which he himself (I
mean the person acting in character of governor)
had issued. I need scarce remind the reader how
happily this alternate state of *authority* and *submission* is exemplified among ourselves.

CHAP. I.

XVIII. Here might be a place to state the different shares which different persons may have in
the issuing the same command: to explain the
nature of *corporate action:* to enumerate and distinguish half a dozen or more different modes in
which *subordination* between the same parties may
subsist: to distinguish and explain the different
senses of the words, "*consent*," "*representation*,"
and others of connected import: *consent,* and *representation;* those interesting but perplexing words,
sources of so much debate: and sources or pre-
texts of so much animosity. But the limits of the
present design will by no means admit of such pro-
tracted and intricate discussions.

Hints of seve-
ral topics
that must be
passed by.

CHAP. I.   **XIX.** In the same manner, also, it may be conceived, how the same set of men considered *among*
The same *themselves*, may at one time be in a state of nature,
society, alter-
nately, in a at another time in a state of government. For the
state of na-
ture and a habit of obedience, in whatever degree of perfection
state of
government. it be necessary it should subsist in order to constitute a government, may be conceived, it is plain, to
suffer interruptions. At different junctures it may
take place and cease.

Instance—   **XX.** Instances of this state of things appear not
the Abori-
gines of to be unfrequent. The sort of society that has been
America.
observed to subsist among the AMERICAN INDIANS
may afford us one. According to the accounts we
have of those people, in most of their tribes, if not
in all, the habit we are speaking of appears to be
taken up only in time of war. It ceases again in
time of peace. The necessity of acting in concert
against a common enemy, subjects a whole tribe to
the orders of a common Chief. On the return of
peace each warrior resumes his pristine independence.

Character-   **XXI.** One difficulty there is that still sticks by
istic of politi-
cal union. us. It has been started indeed, but not solved.—
This is to find a note of distinction,—a characteristic mark, whereby to distinguish a society in
which there *is* a habit of obedience, and that at the

degree of perfection which is necessary to constitute a state of government, from a society in which
there is *not*: a mark, I mean, which shall have a
visible determinate commencement; insomuch that
the instance of its first appearance shall be distinguishable from the last at which it had not as
yet appeared. 'Tis only by the help of such a mark
that we can be in a condition to determine, at any
given time, whether any given society is in a state
of government, or in a state of nature.   I can find
no such mark, I must confess, any where, unless it
be this; the establishment of names of office: the
appearance of a certain man or set of men, with a
certain name, serving to mark them out as objects
of obedience: such as King, Sachem, Cacique, Se-
nator, Burgo-master, and the like.   This, I think,
may serve tolerably well to distinguish a set of men
in a state of political union among *themselves* from
the *same* set of men not yet in such a state.

XXII. But suppose an incontestible political so- Among persons already
ciety, and that a large one, formed; and from that in a state of
political
a smaller body to break off: by this breach the union, at
what instant
smaller body ceases to be in a state of political a new society can be
union with respect to the larger: and has thereby formed, by
defection
placed itself, with respect to that larger body, in a from a former.
state of nature—What means shall we find of ascer-
taining the precise juncture at which this change
took place? What shall be taken for the *character-*

CHAP. I. *istic mark* in this case ? The appointment, it may be
said, of new governors with new names. But no
such appointment, suppose, takes place. The subordinate governors, from whom alone the people at
large were in use to receive their commands under
the old government, are the same from whom they
receive them under the new one. The habit of obedience which these subordinate governors were in
with respect to that single person, we will say, who
was the supreme governor of the whole, is broken
off insensibly and by degrees. The old names by
which these subordinate governors were characterized, while they were subordinate, are continued
now they are supreme. In this case it seems rather
difficult to answer.

First, in case
of defection
by whole
bodies—in-
stance the
Dutch pro-
vinces.

XXIII. If an example be required, we may take
that of the DUTCH provinces with respect to SPAIN.
These provinces were once branches of the Spanish
monarchy. They have now, for a long time, been
universally spoken of as independent states : independent as well of that of Spain as of every other.
They are now in a state of nature with respect to
Spain. They were once in a state of political union
with respect to Spain : namely, in a state of subjection to a single *governor*, a King, who was King
of Spain. At what precise juncture did the dissolution of this political union take place ? At what
precise time did these provinces cease to be subject

to the King of Spain? This, I doubt, will be rather CHAP. I.
difficult to agree upon [e].

XXIV. Suppose the defection to have begun, not 2nd. In
by entire provinces, as in the instance just men- fection by
tioned, but by a handful of fugitives, this augmented Instances,
by the accession of other fugitives, and so, by de- Venice.
grees, to a body of men too strong to be reduced,
the difficulty will be encreased still farther. At
what precise juncture was it that ancient ROME,
or that modern VENICE, became an independent
state?

XXV. In general then, At what precise juncture A *revolt*, at
is it, that persons subject to a government, become, ture it can be
by disobedience, with respect to that government, taken place.
in a state of nature? When is it, in short, that a *re-*
volt shall be deemed to have taken place; and
when, again, is it, that that revolt shall be deemed
to such a degree successful, as to have settled into
independence ?

XXVI. As it is the obedience of individuals that *Disobediences*
constitutes a state of submission, so is it their dis- amount to a
obedience that must constitute a state of revolt. Is

[e] Upon recollection, I have some doubt whether this example
would be found historically exact. If not, that of the defection
of the Nabobs of Indostan may answer the purpose. My first
choice fell upon the former; supposing it to be rather better
known.

CHAP. I. it then every act of disobedience that will do as
much ? The affirmative, certainly, is what can never
be maintained : for then would there be no such
thing as government to be found any where. Here
then a distinction or two obviously presents itself.
Disobedience may be distinguished into *conscious*,
or *unconscious :* and that, with respect as well to
the *law* as to the *fact* [*f*]. Disobedience that is unconscious with respect to either, will readily, I suppose, be acknowledged not to be a revolt. Disobedience again that is conscious with respect to
both, may be distinguished into *secret* and *open ;* or,
in other words, into *fraudulent* and *forcible* [*g*]. Dis-

Disobedience
unconscious
with respect
to the *fact*.

[*f*] 1. Disobedience may be said to be *unconscious with respect
to the fact*, when the party is ignorant either of his having done
the act itself, which is forbidden by the law, or else of his having
done it in those *circumstances*, in which alone it is forbidden.

Disobedience
unconscious
with respect
to the Law.

2. Disobedience may be said to be *unconscious*, with respect to
the *law ;* when although he may know of his having done the *act*
that is in reality forbidden, and that under the *circumstances* in
which it is forbidden, he knows not of its being forbidden, or at
least of its being forbidden in these *circumstances*.

Illustration.

3. So long as the business of spreading abroad the knowledge
of the law continues to lie in the neglect in which it has lain hitherto, instances of disobedience *unconscious with respect to the law*,
can never be otherwise than abundant.

Disobedi-
ences*fraudu-
lent* and *for-
cible*---the
difference, il-
lustrated.

[*g*] If examples be thought necessary, Theft may serve for an
example of *fraudulent* disobedience; Robbery of *forcible*. In
Theft, the *person* of the disobedient party, and the *act* of disobedience, are both endeavoured to be kept secret. In Robbery, the
act of disobedience, at least, if not the *person* of him who disobeys,
is manifest and avowed.

obedience that is only fraudulent, will likewise, I
suppose, be readily acknowledged not to amount
to a revolt.

XXVII. The difficulty that will remain will con- *Disobedi-ences* what *do* *amount* to a *revolt.*
cern such disobedience only as is both *conscious,*
(and that as well with respect to *law* as *fact*,) and
forcible. This disobedience, it should seem, is to
be determined neither by *numbers* altogether (that
is of the persons supposed to be disobedient) nor
by *acts,* nor by *intentions:* all three may be fit to be
taken into consideration. But having brought the
difficulty to this point, at this point I must be content to leave it. To proceed any farther in the endeavour to solve it, would be to enter into a discussion of particular local jurisprudence. It would
be entering upon the definition of Treason, as distinguished from Murder, Robbery, Riot, and other
such crimes, as, in comparison with Treason, are
spoken of as being of a more private nature. Suppose the definition of Treason settled, and the commission of an act of Treason is, as far as regards the
person committing it, the characteristic mark we
are in search of.

XXVIII. These remarks it were easy to extend *Unfinished* *state of the* *above hints.*
to a much greater length. Indeed, it is what would
be necessary, in order to give them a proper full-
ness, and method, and precision. But that could

CHAP. I. not be done without exceeding the limits of the present design. As they are, they may serve as hints to such as shall be disposed to give the subject a more exact and regular examination.

Our Author's
proposition,
" That go-
" vernment
" results of
" course,"
not true.

XXIX. From what has been said, however, we may judge what truth there is in our Author's observation, that " when society" (understand *natural* society) " is once formed, government" (that is political society) (whatever quantity or degree of Obedience is necessary to constitute political society) " results *of course*; as necessary to preserve and to " keep that society in order." By the words, " *of* " *course*," is meant, I suppose, *constantly* and *immediately*; at least constantly. According to this, political society, in any sense of it, ought long ago to have been established all the world over. Whether this be the case, let any one judge from the instances of the Hottentots, of the Patagonians, and of so many other barbarous tribes, of which we hear from travellers and navigators.

Ambiguity
of the sen-
tence.

XXX. It may be, after all, we have misunderstood his meaning. We have been supposing him to have been meaning to assert a *matter of fact*, and to have written, or at least begun, this sentence in the character of an *historical observer :* whereas, all he meant by it, perhaps, was to speak in the character of a *Censor*, and, on a case supposed, to express a

sentiment of approbation. In short, what he meant,
perhaps, to persuade us of, was not that " govern-
" ment" *does actually* " result" from natural " so-
" ciety;" but that it were better that it *should;* to
wit, as being necessary to "preserve and keep" men
" in that state of order," in which it is of advantage
to them that they should be. Which of the above-
mentioned characters he meant to speak in, is a
problem.I must leave to be determined. The distinction, perhaps, is what never so much as occured
to him; and indeed the shifting insensibly, and
without warning, from one of those characters to
the other, is a failing that seems inveterate in our
Author; and of which we shall probably have more
instances than one to notice.

XXXI. To consider the whole paragraph (with Darkness of the whole pa- ragraph fur- ther shewn.
its appendage) together, something, it may be seen,
our Author struggles to overthrow, and something
to establish. But *how* it is he would overthrow, or
what it is he would establish, are questions I must
confess myself unable to resolve. " The preserva-
" tion of mankind," he observes, " was effected by
" single families." This is what, upon the authority
of the Holy Scriptures, he assumes; and from this
it is that he would have us conclude the notion of
an original contract (the same notion which he
afterwards adopts) to be ridiculous. The force of
this conclusion, I must own, I do not see. Man-

kind was preserved by single families—Be it so. What is there in this to hinder "individuals" of those families, or of families descended from those families from meeting together " afterwards in a " large plain," or any where else, " entering into " an *original* contract," or any other contract, " and " choosing the tallest man," or any other man, " present," or absent, to be their Governor? The " flat contradiction" our Author finds between this supposed transaction and the " preservation of " mankind by single families," is what I must own myself unable to discover. As to the " actually " existing unconnected state of nature" he speaks of, " the notion of which," he says, " is too wild to " be seriously admitted," whether this be the case with it, is what, as he has given us no notion of it at all, I cannot judge of.

XXXII. Something positive, however, in one place, we seem to have. These " single families," by which the preservation of mankind was effected; these single families, he gives us to understand, " formed the first society." This is something to proceed upon. A society then of one kind or the other; a natural society, or else a political society, was formed. I would here then put a case, and then propose a question. In this society, we will say no *contract* had as yet been entered into; no *habit of obedience* as yet formed. Was this then a *natural*

society merely, or was it a *political* one? For my CHAP. I.
part, according to my notion of the two kinds of
society as above explained, I can have no difficulty.
It was a merely *natural* one. But, according to our
Author's notion, which was it? If it *was* already a
political one, what notion would he give us of such
an one as shall have been a *natural* one; and by
what change could such precedent natural one have
turned into *this* political one? If this was *not* a
political one, then what sort of a Society are we to
understand any one to be which *is* political? By
what mark are we to distinguish it from a natural
one? To this, it is plain, our Author has not given
any answer. At the same time, that to give an answer to it, was, if any thing, the professed purpose
of the long paragraph before us.

XXXIII. It is time this passage of our Author A general
were dismissed—As among the expressions of it are character.
some of the most striking of those which the voca-
bulary of the subject furnishes, and these ranged
in the most harmonious order, on a distant glance
nothing can look fairer: a prettier piece of tinsel-
work one should seldom see exhibited from the
shew-glass of political erudition. Step close to it
and the delusion vanishes. It is then seen to consist
partly of self-evident observations, and partly of
contradictions; partly of what every one knows already, and partly of what no one can understand.

CHAP. I.   XXXIV. Throughout the whole of it, what dis-

tresses me is, not meeting with any positions, such
as, thinking them false, I find a difficulty in proving them so : but the not meeting with any positions,
true or false, (unless it be here and there a self-evident one,) that I can find a meaning for.   If I can
find nothing positive to accede to, no more can I to
contradict.   Of this latter kind of work, indeed,
there is the less to do for any one else, our Author
himself having executed it, as we have seen, so
amply.

The whole of it is, I must confess, to me a riddle :
more acute, by far, than I am, must be the Oedipus
that can solve it.   Happily it is not necessary, on
account of any thing that follows, that it should
be solved. Nothing is concluded from it. For aught
I can find, it has in itself no use, and none is made
of it. There it is, and as well might it be any where
else, or no where.

XXXV. Were it then possible, there would be
no use in its being solved : but being, as I take it,
really unsolvable, it were of use it should *be seen* to
be so.   Peace may, by this means, be restored to
the breast of many a desponding student, who,
now prepossessed with the hopes of a rich harvest
of instruction, makes a crime to himself of his
inability to reap what, in truth, his Author has not
sown.

XXXVI. As to the Original Contract, by turns embraced and ridiculed by our Author, a few pages, perhaps, may not be ill bestowed in endeavouring to come to a precise notion about its reality and use. The stress laid on it formerly, and still, perhaps, by some, is such as renders it an object not undeserving of attention. I was in hopes, however, till I observed the notice taken of it by our Author, that this chimera had been effectually demolished by Mr. HUME [h]. I think we hear not so much of it

Original Contract a fiction.

[h] 1. In the third Volume of his TREATISE on HUMAN NATURE.

Notion of the Original Contract overthrown by Mr. Hume.

Our Author, one would think, had never so much as opened that celebrated book : of which the criminality in the eyes of some, and the merits in the eyes of others, have since been almost effaced by the splendor of more recent productions of the same pen. The magnanimity of our Author scorned, perhaps, or his circumspection feared, to derive instruction from an enemy : or, what is still more probable, he knew not that the subject had been so much as touched upon by that penetrating and acute metaphysician, whose works lie so much out of the beaten track of Academic reading. But here, as it happens, there is no matter for such fears. Those men who are most alarmed at the dangers of a free enquiry ; those who are most intimately convinced that the surest way to truth is by hearing nothing but on one side, will, I dare answer almost, find nothing of that which they deem poison in this third volume. I would not wish to send the reader to any other than this, which, if I recollect aright, stands clear of the objections that have of late been urged, with so much vehemence, against the work in general*. As to the two first, the Author himself, I am inclined

* By Dr. BEATTIE, in his *Essay on the Immutability of Truth.*

D

CHAP. I. now as formerly. The indestructible prerogatives of
mankind have no need to be supported upon the
sandy foundation of a fiction.

to think, is not ill-disposed, at present, to join with those who are
of opinion, that they might, without any great loss to the science
of Human Nature, be dispensed with. The like might be said,
perhaps, of a considerable part, even of this. But after all re-
trenchments, there will still remain enough to have laid mankind
under indelible obligations. That the foundations of all *virtue* are
laid in *utility*, is there demonstrated, after a few exceptions made,
with the strongest force of evidence : but I see not, any more than
Helvetius saw, what need there was for the exceptions.

History of
a mind per-
plexed by
Fiction.

2. For my own part, I well remember, no sooner had I read
that part of the work which touches on this subject, than I felt as
if scales had fallen from my eyes. I then, for the first time, learnt
to call the cause of the People the cause of Virtue.

Perhaps a short sketch of the wanderings of a raw but well-
intentioned mind, in its researches after moral truth, may, on this
occasion, be not unuseful : for the history of one mind is the history
of many. The writings of the honest, but prejudiced, Earl of
Clarendon, to whose integrity nothing was wanting, and to whose
wisdom little, but the fortune of living something later ; and the con-
tagion of a monkish atmosphere ; these, and other concurrent causes,
had listed my infant affections on the side of despotism. The Ge-
nius of the place I dwelt in, the authority of the state, the voice of
the Church in her solemn offices; all these taught me to call
Charles a Martyr, and his opponents rebels. I saw innovation,
where indeed innovation, but a glorious innovation, was, in their
efforts to withstand him. I saw falsehood, where indeed falsehood
was, in their disavowals of innovation. I saw selfishness, and an
obedience to the call of passion, in the efforts of the oppressed to
rescue themselves from oppression. I saw strong countenance lent
in the sacred writings to monarchic government ; and none to any

XXXVII. With respect to this, and other fictions, CHAP. I.
there was once a time, perhaps, when they had their Fictions *in*
use. With instruments of this temper, I will not *general* mischievous in
deny but that some political work may have been the present
state of
things.

other. I saw *passive obedience* deep stamped with the seal of the
Christian Virtues of humility and self-denial.

Conversing with Lawyers, I found them full of the virtues of
their Original Contract, as a recipe of sovereign efficacy for recon-
ciling the accidental necessity of resistance with the general duty
of submission. This drug of theirs they administered to me to calm
my scruples. But my unpractised stomach revolted against their
opiate. I bid them open to me that page of history in which the
solemnization of this important contract was recorded. They shrunk
from this challenge; nor could they, when thus pressed, do otherwise than our Author has done, confess the whole to be a fiction.
This, methought, looked ill. It seemed to me the acknowledg-
ment of a bad cause, the bringing a fiction to support it. "To
" prove fiction, indeed," said I, " there is need of fiction; but it is the
" characteristic of truth to need no proof but truth. Have you then
" really any such privilege as that of coining facts? You are spend-
" ing argument to no purpose. Indulge yourselves in the licence
" of supposing that to be true which is not, and as well may you
" suppose that proposition itself to be true, which you wish to
" prove, as that other whereby you hope to prove it." Thus
continued I unsatisfying, and unsatisfied, till I learnt to see
that *utility* was the test and measure of all virtue; of loyalty as
much as any: and that the obligation to minister to general happiness, was an obligation paramount to and inclusive of every other.
Having thus got the instruction I stood in need of, I sat down to
make my profit of it. I bid adieu to the original contract: and I
left it to those to amuse themselves with this rattle, who could
think they needed it.

CHAP. I. done, and that useful work, which, under the then circumstances of things, could hardly have been done with any other. But the season of *Fiction* is now over: insomuch, that what formerly might have been tolerated and countenanced under that name, would, if now attempted to be set on foot, be censured and stigmatized under the harsher appellations of *incroachment* or *imposture*. To attempt to introduce any *new* one, would be *now* a crime: for which reason there is much danger, without any use, in vaunting and propagating such as have been introduced already. In point of political discernment, the universal spread of learning has raised mankind in a manner to a level with each other, in comparison of what they have been in any former time: nor is any man now so far elevated above his fellows, as that he should be indulged in the dangerous licence of cheating them for their good.

This had a momentary use.

XXXVIII. As to the fiction now before us, in the character of an *argumentum ad hominem*, coming when it did, and managed as it was, it succeeded to admiration.

That compacts, by whomsoever entered into, *ought* to be kept;—that men are *bound* by compacts, are propositions which men, without knowing or enquiring why, were disposed universally to accede to. The observance of promises they had been accustomed to see pretty constantly enforced. They had been accustomed to see Kings, as well as others, behave themselves as if bound by them. This pro- position, then, " that men are bound by *compacts;*" and this other, ".that, if one party performs not his " part, the other is released from his," being pro- positions which no man disputed, were propositions which no man had any call to prove. In theory they were assumed for axioms: and in practice they were observed as rules [*i*]. If, on any occasion, it was thought proper to make a shew of proving them, it was rather for form's sake than for any thing else: and that, rather in the way of memento or instruc- tion to acquiescing auditors, than in the way of proof against opponents. On such an occasion the com- mon-place retinue of phrases was at hand; *Justice,* *Right Reason* required it, the *Law* of *Nature* com- manded it, and so forth; all which are but so many ways of intimating that a man is firmly persuaded of the truth of this or that moral proposition, though he either thinks he *need not,* or finds he *can't,* tell *why.* Men were too obviously and too generally interested in the observance of these rules to enter- tain doubts concerning the force of any arguments they saw employed in their support.—It is an old observation how Interest smooths the road to Faith.

[*i*] A *compact* or *contract* (for the two words on this occasion, A *compact,* at least, are used in the same sense) may, I think, be defined a pair or, *contract.* of promises, by two persons reciprocally given, the one promise in consideration of the other.

CHAP. I.

Terms of the supposed contract stated.

XXXIX. A compact, then, it was said, was made by the King and People: the terms of it were to this effect. The People, on their part, promised to the King a *general obedience*. The King, on his part, promised to *govern* the people in such a *particular* manner always, as should be *subservient* to their happiness. I insist not on the words: I undertake only for the sense; as far as an imaginary engagement, so loosely and so variously worded by those who have imagined it, is capable of any decided signification. Assuming then, as a general rule, that promises, when made, ought to be observed; and, as a point of fact, that a promise to this effect in particular had been made by the party in question, men were more ready to deem themselves qualified to judge when it was such a promise was *broken*, than to decide directly and avowedly on the delicate question, when it was that a King acted so far in *opposition* to the happiness of his people, that it were better no longer to obey him.

Stated thus generally, it could not dispense men from entering into the question of *utility*, as was intended

XL. It is manifest, on a very little consideration, that nothing was gained by this manœuvre after all: no difficulty removed by it. It was still necessary, and that as much as ever, that the question men studied to avoid should be determined, in order to determine the question they thought to substitute in its room. It was still necessary to determine, whether the King in question had, or had not acted so far in *opposition* to the happiness of his people, that it were better no longer to obey him; in order to determine, whether the promise he was supposed to have made, had or bad not been broken. For what was the supposed purport of this promise? It was no other than what has just been mentioned.

CHAP. I.

XLI. Let it be said, that part at least of this promise was to govern in *subservience to Law:* that hereby a more precise rule was laid down for his conduct, by means of this supposal of a promise, than that other loose and general rule to govern in subservience to the *happiness of his people:* and that, by this means, it is the letter of the *Law* that forms the tenor of the rule.

Now true it is, that the governing in opposition to Law, is *one* way of governing in opposition to the happiness of the people: the natural effect of such a contempt of the Law being, if not actually to destroy, at least to threaten with destruction, all those rights and privileges that are founded on it: rights and privileges on the enjoyment of which that happiness depends. But still it is not this that can be safely taken for the entire purport of the promise here in question: and that for several reasons. *First,* Because the most mischievous, and under certain constitutions the most feasible, method of governing in opposition to the happiness of the people, is, by setting the Law itself in opposition to their happiness. *Second.* Because it is a case very

CHAP. I. conceivable, that a King may, to a great degree,
impair the happiness of his people without violat-
ing the letter of any single Law. *Third*, Because
extraordinary occasions may now and then occur,
in which the happiness of the people may be better
promoted by acting, for the moment, in *opposition*
to the Law, than in *subservience* to it. *Fourth*,
Because it is not any single violation of the Law,
as such, that can properly be taken for a breach of
his part of the contract, so as to be understood to
have released the people from the obligation of
performing theirs. For, to quit the fiction, and re-
sume the language of plain truth, it is scarce ever
any single violation of the Law that, by being *submitted to*, can produce so much mischief as shall
surpass the probable mischief of *resisting* it. If
every single instance whatever of such a violation
were to be deemed an entire dissolution of the contract, a man who reflects at all would scarce find
any-where, I believe, under the sun, that Government which he could allow to subsist for twenty
years together. It is plain, therefore, that to pass
any sound decision upon the question which the in-
ventors of this fiction substituted instead of the
true one, the latter was still necessary to be decided. All they gained by their contrivance was,
the convenience of deciding it obliquely, as it were,
and by a side wind—that is, in a crude and hasty
way, without any direct and steady examination.

XLII. But, after all, for what *reason* is it, that men *ought* to keep their promises? The moment any intelligible reason is given, it is this: that it is for the *advantage* of society they should keep them; and if they do not, that, as far as *punishment* will go, they should be *made* to keep them. It is for the advantage of the whole number that the promises of each individual should be kept: and, rather than they should not be kept, that such individuals as fail to keep them should be punished. If it be asked, how this appears? the answer is at hand:—Such is the benefit to gain, and mischief to avoid, by keeping them, as much more than compensates the mischief of so much punishment as is requisite to oblige men to it. Whether the dependence of *benefit* and *mischief* (that is, of *pleasure* and *pain*) upon men's conduct in this behalf, be as here stated, is a question of *fact*, to be decided, in the same manner that all other questions of fact are to be decided, by testimony, observation, and experience [*k*].

CHAP. L.

Nor is it an original independent principle.

[*k*] The importance which the observance of promises is of to the happiness of society, is placed in a very striking and satisfactory point of view, in a little apologue of MONTESQUIEU, intitled, *The History of the Troglodytes* *. The Troglodytes are a people who pay no regard to promises. By the natural consequences of this disposition, they fall from one scene of misery into another; and are at last exterminated. The same Philosopher, in

* See the Collection of his Works.

CHAP. I.

Nor can it serve to prove any thing, but what may be better proved without it.

XLIII. This then, and no other, being the *reason* why men should be made to keep their promises, viz. that it is for the advantage of society that they should, is a reason that may as well be given at once, why *Kings*, on the one hand, in governing, should in general keep within established Laws, and (to speak universally) abstain from all such measures as tend to the unhappiness of their subjects: and, on the other hand, why *subjects* should obey Kings as long as they so conduct themselves, and no longer; why they should obey in short *so long as the probable mischiefs of obedience are less than the probable mischiefs of resistance:* why, in a word, taking the whole body together, it is their *duty* to obey, just so long as it is their *interest*, and no longer. This being the case, what need of saying of the one, that *he* PROMISED so to *govern;* of the other, that they PROMISED so to *obey*, when the fact is otherwise?

The Coronation-Oath does not come up to the notion of it.

XLIV. True it is, that, in this country, according to ancient forms, some sort of vague promise of *good government* is made by Kings at the ceremony of their coronation: and let the ac-

his *Spirit of Laws*, copying and refining upon the current jargon, feigns a Law for this and other purposes, after defining a Law to be a *relation*. How much more instructive on this head is the fable of the Troglodytes than the pseudo-metaphysical sophistry of the *Esprit des Loix!*

clamations, perhaps given, perhaps not given, CHAP. I.
by chance persons out of the surrounding multitude, be construed into a promise of *obedience* on
the part of the *whole* multitude : that whole multitude itself, a small drop collected together by
chance out of the ocean of the state: and let the
two promises thus made be deemed to have formed
a perfect *compact* :—not that either of them is declared to be the *consideration* of the other *.

XLV. Make the most of this concession, one The obligation of a pro-
experiment there is, by which every reflecting man mise will not
stand against
may satisfy himself, I think, beyond a doubt, that that of utility:
while that of
it is the consideration of *utility*, and no other, that, utility will
against that
secretly, perhaps, but unavoidably, has governed his of a promise.
judgment upon all these matters. The experiment is
easy and decisive. It is but to reverse, in supposition, in the first place the import of the *particular*
promise thus feigned ; in the next place, the effect
in point of *utility* of the observance of promises *in
general.*—Suppose the King to promise that he
would govern his subjects *not* according to Law;
not in the view to promote their happiness :—would
this be binding upon *him* ? Suppose the people to
promise they would obey him *at all events*, let him
govern as he will; let him govern to their destruction. Would this be binding upon *them* ? Suppose

* V. supra par. 38. note [i].

CHAP. I. the constant and universal effect of an observance
of promises were to produce *mischief*, would it *then*
be men's *duty* to observe them? Would it *then* be
right to make Laws, and apply punishment to *oblige*
men to observe them?

A fallacy ob-
viated.

XLVI. " No;" (it may perhaps be replied) ". but
" for this reason; among promises, some there are
" that, as every one allows, are void : now these
" you have been supposing, are unquestionably of
" the number. A promise that is in itself *void*,
" cannot, it is true, create any obligation : But
" allow the promise to be *valid*, and it is the pro-
" mise itself that creates the obligation, and no-
" thing else." The fallacy of this argument it is
easy to perceive. For what is it then that the promise depends on for its *validity ?* what is it that
being *present* makes it *valid ?* what is it that being
wanting makes it *void ?* To acknowledge that any
one promise may be void, is to acknowledge that
if any *other* is *binding*, it is not merely because it is
a promise. That circumstance then, whatever it
be, on which the validity of a promise depends,
that circumstance, I say, and not the promise itself must, it is plain, be the cause of the obligation which a promise is apt in general to carry
with it.

The obliga-
tion of a pro-

XLVII. But farther. Allow, for argument's sake,

what we have disproved: allow that the obligation of a promise is independent of every other:
allow that a promise is binding *proprid vi*—Binding then on whom? On him certainly who makes
it. Admit this: For what reason is the same individual promise to be binding on those who *never*
made it? The King, *fifty years ago*, promised my
Great-Grandfather to govern him according to
Law: my Great-Grandfather, *fifty years ago*, promised the King to obey him according to Law.
The King, *just now*, promised my *neighbour* to govern him according to Law: my neighbour, *just
now*, promised the King to obey him according to
Law.—Be it so—What are these promises, all or
any of them, to *me?* To make answer to this question, some other principle, it is manifest, must be
resorted to, than that of the *intrinsic* obligation of
promises upon those who make them.

CHAP. I.

mise, were it even *independent*, would not be *extensive* enough for the purpose.

XLVIII. Now this *other* principle that still re-
curs upon us, what other can it be than the *principle of* UTILITY [*l*]? The principle which furnishes

But the principle of *utility* is all-sufficient.

[*l*] To this denomination, has of late been added, or substituted,
the *greatest happiness* or *greatest felicity* principle : this, for shortness, instead of saying at length *that principle* which states the greatest happiness of all those whose interest is in question, as being the
right and proper, and only right and proper and universally de-
sirable, *end* of human action : of human action in every situation ;
and, in particular, in that of a functionary, or set of functionaries,

CHAP. I. us with that *reason*, which alone depends not upon

exercising the powers of Government. The word *utility* does not so clearly point to the ideas of *pleasure* and *pain* as the words *happiness* and *felicity* do: nor does it lead us to the consideration of the *number*, of the interests affected: so the *number*, as being the circumstance which contributes, in the largest proportion, to the formation of the standard here in question; the *standard of right and wrong*, by which alone the propriety of human conduct, in every situation, can with propriety be tried.

This want of a sufficiently manifest connection between the ideas of *happiness* and *pleasure* on the one hand, and the idea of *utility* on the other, I have every now and then found operating, and with but too much efficiency, as a bar to the acceptance, that might otherwise have been given, to this principle.

For further elucidation of the principle of *utility*, or say *greatest happiness principle*, it may be some satisfaction to the reader, to see a note, inserted in a second edition, now printing, of a later work of the Author's, intitled, " *An Introduction to the principles of Morals and Legislation.*" In chapter I. subjoined to paragraph xiii. is a note in these words:—" The principle of utility" (I have heard it said) " is a dangerous principle: it is dangerous on cer-" tain occasions to consult it." This is as much as to say—what? that it is not consonant to utility, to consult utility; in short, that it is *not* consulting it, to consult it.

In the second edition, to this note is added the following paragraph.

Explanation, written 12th July, 1822, relative to the above note.

Not long after the publication of the *Fragment on Government,* Anno 1776, in which, in the character of an all-comprehensive and all-commanding principle, the principle of *utility* was brought to view, one person by whom observation to the above effect was made was *Alexander Wedderburn,* at that time *Attorney* or *Solicitor General,* afterwards successively *Chief Justice of the Common*

any higher reason, but which is itself the sole and

Pleas, and *Chancellor of England,* under the successive titles of
Lord Loughborough and *Earl of Rosslyn.* It was made—not indeed
in my hearing, but in the bearing of a person by whom it was almost immediately communicated to me. So far from being self-con-
tradictory, it was (I now see and confess) a shrewd and perfectly
true one. By that distinguished functionary, the state of the
Government was thoroughly understood; by the obscure individual, at that time, not so much as supposed to be so; his dis-
quisitions had not been as yet applied, with any thing like a comprehensive view, to the field of Constitutional Law, nor therefore
to those features of the English Government, by which the greatest
happiness of the ruling *one,* with or without that of a favoured few,
are now so plainly seen to be the only ends to which the course of
it has at any time been directed. The *principle of utility* was an
appellative, at that time employed—employed by me, as it has
been by others, to designate that which, in a more perspicuous
and instructive manner, may as above be designated by the name
of the *greatest happiness principle.* " This principle" (said Wedderburn) " is a dangerous one." Saying so, he said that which, to
a certain extent, is strictly true; a principle, which lays down, as
the only *right* and justifiable end of Government, the greatest happiness of the greatest number—how can it be denied to be a dangerous one? dangerous to every Government, which has for its
actual end or object, the greatest happiness of a certain *one,* with
or without the addition of some comparatively small number of
others, whom it is matter of pleasure or accommodation to him to
admit, each of them, to a share in the concern, on the footing of
so many junior partners. " *Dangerous*" it therefore really was to
the interest—the sinister interest of all those functionaries, himself
included, whose interest it was to maximize delay, vexation, and expence, in judicial and other modes of procedure, for the sake of
the profit extractible out of the expence. In a Government which

CHAP. I. all-sufficient reason for every point of practice whatsoever.

had for its end in view the greatest happiness of the greatest number, *Alexander Wedderburn* might have been *Attorney General* and *then Chancellor*; but he would not have been Attorney General with 15,000*l.* a year, nor Chancellor, with a Peerage, with a veto upon all justice, with 25,000*l.* a year, and with 500 sinecures at his disposal, under the name of Ecclesiastical Benefices besides *et cæteras* — *Note of the Author's*, 12th July, 1822.

CHAP. II.

FORMS OF GOVERNMENT.

I. THE contents of the whole digression we are examining, were distributed, we may remember, at the outset of this essay, into five divisions. The first, relative to the manner in which Government in general was formed, has already been examined in the preceding chapter. The next, relative to the different *species* or *forms* it may assume, comes now to be considered.

CHAP. II.

Subject of the present chapter.

II. The first object that strikes us in this division of our subject is the theological flourish it sets out with. In God may be said, though in a peculiar sense, to be our Author's strength. In theology he has found a not unfrequent source, of ornament to divert us, of authority to overawe us, from sounding into the shallowness of his doctrines [a].

Theological flourish of our Author.

III. That governors, of some sort or other, we must have, is what he has been shewing in the

Governors— celestial endowments found for them.

[a] This is what there would be occasion to shew at large, were what he says of LAW in *general*, and of the LAWS of *Nature* and *Revelation* in particular, to be examined.

E

CHAP. II. manner we have seen in the last chapter. Now for *endowments* to qualify them for the exercise of their function. These endowments then, as if it were to make them shew the brighter, and to keep them, as much as possible, from being soiled by the rough hands of impertinent speculators, he has chosen should be of æthereal texture, and has fetched them from the clouds.

" All mankind *," he says, " will agree that go-" vernment should be reposed in such persons in " whom those qualities are most likely to be found, " the perfection of which are among the attributes " of Him who is emphatically styled the Supreme " Being: the three great requisites, I mean, of " wisdom, of goodness, and of power."

But let us see the whole passage as it stands—

The passage recited.

IV. " But as all the members of Society," (mean-ing *natural* Society) " are naturally EQUAL," (*i. e.* I suppose, with respect to *political* power, of which none of them as yet have any) " it may be asked." (continues he) " in whose hands are the reins of " government to be intrusted ? To this the general " answer is easy ; but the application of it to par-" ticular cases, has occasioned one half of those " mischiefs which are apt to proceed from mis-" guided political zeal. In general, all mankind

1. Comm. p. 48.

" will agree that government should be reposed in CHAP. II.
" such persons in whom those qualities are most
" likely to be found; the perfection of which are
" among the attributes of Him who is emphatically
" styled the Supreme Being; the three grand re-
" quisites, I mean, of wisdom, goodness, and of
" power; wisdom, to discern the real interest of
" the community; goodness, to endeavour always
" to pursue that real interest; and strength or
" power, to carry this knowledge and intention into
" action. These are the natural foundations of so-
" vereignty, and these are the requisites that ought
" to be found in every well constituted frame of go-
" vernment."

V. Every thing in its place. Theology in a ser- Theology on
mon, or a catechism. But in this place, the flourish such an occasion as this
we have seen, might, for every purpose of instruc- impertinent.
tion, have much better, it should seem, been spared.
What purpose the idea of that tremendous and
incomprehensible Being thus unnecessarily introduced can answer, I cannot see unless it were to
bewilder and entrance the reader; as it seems to
have bewildered and entranced the writer. Beginning thus, is beginning at the wrong end: it is
explaining *ignotum per ignotius*. It is not from the
attributes of the Deity, that an idea is to be had of
any qualities in men: on the contrary, it is from
what we see of the qualities of men, that we obtain

CHAP. II. the feeble idea we can frame to ourselves, of the attributes of the Deity.

Difficulty it leads him into.

VI. We shall soon see whether it be light or darkness our Author has brought back from this excursion to the clouds. The qualifications he has pitched upon for those in whose hands Government is to be reposed, we see are *three* : wisdom, goodness, and power. Now of these three, one there is which, I doubt, will give him some trouble to know what to do with. I mean, that of *Power:* which, looking upon it as a jewel, it should seem, that would give a lustre to the royal diadem, he was for importing from the celestial regions. In heaven, indeed, we shall not dispute its being to be found; and that at all junctures alike. But the parallel, I doubt, already fails. In the earthly governors in question, or, to speak more properly, candidates for government, by the very supposition there can not, at the juncture he supposes, be any such thing. *Power* is that very quality which, in consideration of these other qualities, which, it is supposed, are possessed by them already, they are now waiting to receive.

Power, either natural or political.

VII. By Power in this place, I, for my part, mean *political* power: the only sort of power our Author could mean: the only sort of power that is here in question. A little farther on we shall find

him speaking of this endowment as being possessed, and that in the highest degree, by a King,
a single person. *Natural* power therefore, mere
organical power, the faculty of giving the hardest
blows, can never, it is plain, be that which he meant
to number among the attributes of this godlike
personage.

VIII. We see then the dilemma our Author's *In neither sense can it be attributed as he attributes it.*
theology has brought him into, by putting him upon
reckoning *power* among the qualifications of his
candidates. Power is either *natural* or *political*.
Political power is what they cannot have by the
supposition : for that is the very thing that is to be
created, and which, by the establishment of Government, men are going to confer on them. If
any then, it must be *natural* power ; the natural
strength that a man possesses of himself without
the help of Government. But of this then, if this
be it, there is more, if we may believe our Author,
in a single member of a society, than in that member and all the rest of the society put together [b].

IX. This difficulty, if possible, one should be *What it is that may.*
glad to see cleared up. The truth is, I take it,

[b] V. infra, par. 32. Monarchy, which is the government of
one, " is the most powerful form of government," he says, " of
any :" more so than Democracy, which he describes as being the
Government of *all.*

CHAP. II. that in what our Author has said of power, he has
been speaking, as it were, by anticipation; and
that what he means by it, is not any power of either
kind actually possessed by any man, or body of
men, at the juncture he supposes, but only a *capacity*, if one may call it so, of *retaining* and *putting* into action political power, whensoever it shall
have been conferred. Now, of actual power, the
quantity that is possessed is, in every case, one
and the same: for it is neither more nor less than
the supreme power. But as to the capacity above
spoken of, there do seem, indeed, to be good
grounds for supposing it to subsist in a higher
degree in a *single* man than in a *body*.

—and for
what reason.
X. These grounds it will not be expected that I
should display at large: a slight sketch will be
sufficient.—The efficacy of power is, in part at
least, in proportion to the promptitude of obedience: the promptitude of obedience is, in part, in
proportion to the promptitude of command:—command is an expression of will: a will is sooner
formed by one than many. And this, or something like it, I take to be the plain English of our
Author's metaphor, where he tells us *, as we shall
see a little farther on †, that " a monarchy is the
" most powerful" [form of government] " of any, all

* Comm. p. 50.   † Par. 32.

" the sinews of government being knit together, CHAP. II.
" and united in the hands of the prince."

XI. The next paragraph, short as it is, contains Heteroge-
neous con-
variety of matter. The first two sentences of it are tents of the
next para-
to let us know, that with regard to the manner in graph.
which the *particular* governments that we know
of have been formed, he thinks proper to pass it
by. A third is to intimate, for the second time,
that all Governments must be absolute in some
hands or other: In the fourth and last, he favours
us with a very comfortable piece of intelligence;
the truth of which, but for his averment, few of us
perhaps would have suspected. This is, that the
qualifications mentioned by the last paragraph as
requisite to be possessed by all Governors of states
are, or at least once upon a time were, *actually*
possessed by them: (i. e.) according to the opinion
of somebody; but of what somebody is not altogether clear: whether in the opinion of these Governors themselves, or of the persons governed by
them.

XII. " How the several forms of Government we The paragraph recited.
" now see in the world at first actually began,"
says our Author, " is matter of great uncertainty,
" and has occasioned infinite disputes. It is not
" my business or intention to enter into any of

CHAP. II. " them.   However they began, or by what right
" soever they subsist, there is and must be in all of
" them a supreme, irresistable, absolute, uncon-
" trolled authority, in which the *jura summi im-*
" *perii,* or the rights of sovereignty reside.   And
" this authority is placed in those hands, wherein
" (according to the OPINION of the FOUNDERS of
" such respective states, either expressly given or
" collected from their *tacit* APPROBATION) the qua-
" lities requisite for supremacy, wisdom, goodness,
" and power, are the most likely to be found."

Paradoxical
assertion in
the latter
part of it, as
if all govern-
ments were
the result of
a free prefer-
ence

XIII. Who those persons are whom our Author
means here by the word *founders;* whether those
who became the Governors of the states in question,
or those who became the governed, or both together, is what I would not take upon me positively
to determine.   For aught I know he may have
meant neither the one nor the other, but some third
person.   And, indeed, what I am vehemently inclined to suspect is, that, in our Author's large
conception, the mighty and extensive domains of
ATHENS and SPARTA, of which we read so much
at school and at college, consisting each of several
score of miles square, represented, at the time this
paragraph was writing, the whole universe: and the
respective æras of *Solon* and *Lycurgus,* the whole
period of the history of those states.

XIV. The words " founders,"—" opinion,"— CHAP. II.
" approbation,"—in short, the whole complection

Reasons for
supposing
this to have
been the
meaning of it.

of the sentence is such as brings to one's view a
system of government utterly different from the
generality of those we have before our eyes : a system in which one would think neither caprice, nor
violence, nor accident, nor prejudice, nor passion,
had any share : a system uniform, comprehensive,
and simultaneous; planned with phlegmatic deli-
beration; established by full and general assent:
such, in short, as, according to common imagination, were the systems laid down by the two sages
abovementioned. If this be the case, the object he
had in mind when he said *Founders*, might be neither Govern*ors* nor govern*ed*, but some *neutral*
person: such as those sages, chosen as they were
in a manner as umpires, might be considered with
regard to the persons who, under the prior constitution, whatever it was, had stood respectively
in those two relations.

XV. All this, however, is but conjecture : in the

proposition itself neither this, nor any other restriction is expressed. It is delivered explicitly and emphatically in the character of an universal one. "In
" ALL OF THEM," he assures us, " this authority,"
(the supreme authority) " *is* placed in those hands,
" wherein, according to the *opinion* of the *founders*
" of such respective states," these " qualities of

CHAP. II.

*—applied to
particular
instances.*

" wisdom, goodness, and power, are the most likely
" to be found." In this character it cannot but
throw a singular light on history. I can see no end,
indeed, to the discoveries it leads to, all of them
equally new and edifying. When the Spaniards, for
example, became masters of the empire of Mexico,
a vulgar politician might suppose it was because
such of the Mexicans as remained unexterminated,
could not help it. No such thing—It was because
either the Spaniards were of "opinion," or the
Mexicans themselves were of "opinion" (which of
the two is altogether clear) that, in Charles Vth, and
his successors, more goodness (of which they had
such abundant proofs) as well as wisdom, was likely
to be found, than in all the Mexicans put together.
The same persuasion obtained between Charlemagne
and the German Saxons with respect to the goodness and wisdom of Charlemagne:—between William the Norman and the English Saxons:—between Mahomet IId and the subjects of John Pale-
ologus:—between Odoacer and those of Augus-
tulus:—between the Tartar Gingiskan and the
Chinese of his time:—between the Tartars Chang-ti
and Cam-ghi, and the Chinese of their times:—between the Protector Cromwell and the Scotch:—
between William IIId and the Irish Papists:—between Cæsar and the Gauls:—in short, between
the Thirty Tyrants, so called, and the Athenians,
whom our Author seems to have had in view:—to

mention these examples only, out of as many hun-
dred as might be required. All this, if we may
trust our Author, he has the "*goodness*" to believe:
and by such lessons is the penetration of students
to be sharpened for piercing into the depths of
politics.

XVI. So much for the introductory paragraph.— General
contents of
The main part of the subject is treated of in six the six remaining para-
others: the general contents of which are as graphs relating to the
subject of
follows. this chapter.

XVII. In the first he tells us how many different —of the first
paragraph..
forms of government there are according to the division of the ancients; which division he adopts.
These are three: Monarchy, Aristocracy, and Democracy.

XVIII. The next is to tell us, that by the *sove-* —Second.—
reign POWER he means that of "*making laws.*"

XIX. In a third he gives us the advantages and —Third.—
disadvantages of these three different forms of
government.

XX. In a fourth he tells us that these are all the —Fourt :.—
antients would allow of.

XXI. A fifth is to tell us that the British form of —Fifth.—

CHAP. II. Government is different from each of them; being a
combination of all, and possessing the advantages
of all.

XXII. In the sixth, and last, he shews us that it
could not possess these advantages, if, instead of
being what it is, it were either of those others: and
tells us what it is that may destroy it. These two
last it will be sufficient here to mention: to examine
them will be the task of our next chapter.

Definitions
of the three
sorts of
governments
according to
our Author.   XXIII. Monarchy is that form of Government in
which the power of making Laws is lodged in the
hands of a *single* member of the state in question.
Aristocracy is that form of Government in which the
power of making laws is lodged in the hands of
several members.   Democracy is that form of government in which the power of making laws is
lodged in the hands of "*all*" of them put together.
These, according to our Author, are the definitions
of the Antients; and these, therefore, without difficulty, are the definitions of our Author.

XXIV. " The political writers of antiquity," says
he, " will not allow more than three regular forms
" of government; the first, when the sovereign
" power is lodged in an aggregate assembly, con-
" sisting of all the members of a community which
" is called a Democracy; the second, when it is

" lodged in a council composed of select members, CHAP. II.
" and then it is styled an Aristocracy; the last,
" when it is entrusted in the hands of a single
" person, and then it takes the name of a Monarchy.
" All other species of government they say are
" either corruptions of, or reducible to these three."

XXV. " By the sovereign power, as was before and the next.
" observed, is meant the making of laws; for wher-
" ever that power resides, all others must conform
" to, and be directed by it, whatever appearance
" the outward form and administration of the go-
" vernment may put on. For it is at any time in
" the option of the legislature to alter that form
" and administration by a new edict or rule, and to
" put the execution of the laws into whatever hands
" it pleases: and all the other powers of the state
" must obey the legislative power in the execution
" of their several functions, or else the constitution
" is at an end."

XXVI. Having thus got three regular simple How he as-
signs them
forms of Government (this anomalous complex one their respec-
tive qualifi-
of our own out of the question) and just as many cations.---
qualifications to divide among them; of each of
which, by what he told us a while ago, each form of
Government must have some share, it is easy to see
how their allotments will be made out. Each form
of Government will possess one of these qualities

CHAP. II. in perfection, taking its chance, if one may say so, for its share in the two others.

All appearing equally eli-gible in his view of them.

XXVII. Among these three different forms of Government then, it should seem, according to our Author's account of them, there is not much to choose. Each of them has a *qualification*, an *endowment*, to itself. Each of them is completely characterized by this qualification. No intimation is given of any pre-eminence among these qualifications, one above another. Should there be any dispute concerning the preference to be given to any of these forms of Government, as proper a method as any of settling it, to judge from this view of them, is that of cross and pile. Hence we may infer, that all the Governments that ever were, or will be, (except a very particular one that we shall come to presently, that is to say, our own) are upon a par: that of ATHENS with that of PERSIA; that that of GENEVA with that of MOROCCO; since they are all of them, he tells us, " corruptions of, or reducible to," one of these. This is happy. A legislator cannot do amiss. He may save himself the expence of thinking. The choice of a King was once determined, we are told, by the neighing of a horse. The choice of a form of Government might be determined so as well.

—How to the

XXVIII. As to our own form of Government,

however, this, it is plain, being that which it seemed good to take for the theme of his panegyric, and being made out of the other three, will possess the advantages of all of them put together; and that without any of the disadvantages; the disadvantages vanishing at the word of command, or even without it, as not being suitable to the purpose.

CHAP. II.
~
British Constitution.

XXIX. At the end of the paragraph which gives us the above definitions, one observation there is that is a little puzzling. " Other species of government," we are given to understand, there are besides these; but then those others, if not " reducible to," are but " corruptions of these." Now, what there is in any of these to be corrupted, is not so easy to understand. The essence of these several forms of government, we must always remember, is placed by him, solely and entirely, in the article of *number :* in the ratio of the number of the Governors, (for so for shortness we will style those in whose hands is lodged this " power of " making laws") to that of the govern*ed*. If the number of the former be, to that of the latter, as *one* to *all*, then is the form of Government a Monarchy : if as *all* to *all*, then is it a Democracy : if as some number *between one and all*, to *all*, then is it an Aristocracy. Now then, if we can conceive a fourth number, which not being more than all, is neither one nor all, nor any thing between one and

Contradiction he falls into, in supposing other sorts of Government than these three, described as they are by him.

CHAP. II. all, we can conceive a form of Government, which,
upon due proof, may appear to be a corruption of
some one or other of these three [c]. If not, we
must look for the corruption somewhere else: Suppose it were in our Author's *reason* [d].

Governments
the same as
these under
other names.

XXX. Not but that we may meet, indeed, with
several other hard-worded names for forms of Government: but these names were only so many
names for one or other of those three. We hear
often of a *Tyranny:* but this is neither more nor
less than the name a man gives to our Author's
Monarchy, when out of humour with it. · It is still·
the Government of number *one.* We hear now and
then too, of a sort of Government called an *Oli-*

---

[c] By the laws of GERMANY, such and such states are to furnish so many men to the general army of the Empire: some of
them so many men and one half; others, so many and one third:
others again, if I mistake not, so many and one fourth. One of
these half-, third part, or quarter-men, suppose, possesses himself
of the Government: here then we have a kind of corruption of a
Monarchy. Is this what our Author had in view?

[d] A more suitable place to look for *corruption* in, if we may
take his own word for it, there cannot be. " Every man's rea-
" son," he assures us *, " is corrupt;" and not only that, but " his
" understanding full of ignorance and error."—With regard to
others, it were as well not to be too positive; but with regard to a
man's self, what he tells us from experience, it would be ill manners to dispute with him.

* 1 Comm. p. 41.

garchy : but this is neither more nor less than the CHAP. II.
name a man gives to our Author's Aristocracy, in
the same case. It is still the Government of some
number or other, *between one and all.* In fine, we
hear now and then of a sort of Government fit to
break one's teeth, called an *Ochlocracy :* but this is
neither more nor less than the name a man gives to
a Democracy in the same case. It is still that sort
of Government, which, according to our Author, is
the Government of *all.*

XXXI. Let us now see how he has disposed of his three qualifications among his three sorts or forms of Government. Upon Monarchy, we shall find, he has bestowed the perfection of power; on Aristocracy, of wisdom; on Democracy, of goodness : each of these forms having just enough, we may suppose, of the two remaining qualifications besides its own peculiar one, to make up the necessary complement of "qualities requisite for supremacy." Kings are, (nay *were* before they were Kings, since it was this qualification determined their subjects to make them Kings*) as strong as so many Hercules's ; but then, as to their wisdom, or their goodness, there is not much to say. The members of an Aristocracy are so many Solomons : but then they are not such sturdy folks as your Kings; nor, if the truth is to be spoken, have they

Qualifications of the three forms, how allotted---the subject resumed.

* 1 Comm. p. 48.

CHAP. II. much more honesty than their neighbours. As to the members of a Democracy, they are the best sort of people in the world; but then they are but a puny sort of gentry, as to strength, put them all together; and apt to be a little defective in point of understanding.

The paragraph recited.

XXXII. "In a democracy," says he, "where the "right of making laws resides in the people at "large, public virtue or goodness of intention, is "more likely to be found, than either of the other "qualities of government. Popular assemblies are "frequently foolish in their contrivance, and weak "in their execution; but generally mean to do the "thing that is right and just, and have always a "degree of patriotism or public spirit. In aris- "tocracies there is more wisdom to be found than "in the other frames of Government; being com- "posed, or intended to be composed, of the most "experienced citizens; but there is less honesty "than in a republic, and less strength than in a "monarchy. A monarchy is indeed the most "powerful of any, all the sinews of government "being knit together and united in the hand of the "prince; but then there is imminent danger of his "employing that strength to improvident or op- "pressive purposes."

—and the next.

XXXIII. "Thus these three species of govern-

" ment have all of them their several perfections CHAP. II.
" and imperfections. Democracies are usually the
" best calculated to direct the end of a law; aris-
" tocracies to invent the means by which that end
" shall be obtained; and monarchies to carry those
" means into execution. And the antients, as was
" observed, had in general no idea of any other
" permanent form of government but these three;
" for though Cicero declares himself of opinion,
" *esse optimè constitutam rempublicam, quæ ex tribus*
" *generibus illis, regali, optimo, et populari sit modicè*
" *confusa;* yet Tacitus treats this notion of a mixed
" government, formed out of them all, and par-
" taking of the advantages of each, as a visionary
" whim; and one, that if effected, could never be
" lasting or secure."

XXXIV. In the midst of this fine-spun ratiocina- Democracy, as described
tion, an accident has happened, of which our Author by him, no Government
seems not to be aware. One of his *accidents*, as a at all.
logician would say, has lost its *subject:* one of the
qualifications he has been telling us of, is, somehow
or other, become vacant: the form of Government
he designed it for, having unluckily slipped through
his fingers in the handling. I mean Democracy;
which he, and, according to him, the Antients,
make out to be the government of *all.* Now "*all*"
is a great many; so many that, I much doubt, it
will be rather a difficult matter to find these high

CHAP. II. and mighty personages power enough, so much as

Democracy, as described by him, no Government at all.

to make a decent figure with. The members of this
redoubtable Commonwealth will be still worse off,
I doubt, in point of subjects, than *Trinculo* in the
play, or than the potentates, whom some late
navigators found lording it, with might and main,
" ϰϱατεϱῃϕι βιηϕι," over a Spanish settlement: there
were three members of the Government; and they
had one subject among them all * [e].   Let him
examine it a little, and it will turn out, I take it, to
be precisely that sort of Government, and no other,
which one can conceive to obtain, where there is no
Government at all.   Our Author, we may remember, had shrewd doubts about the existence of a
state of nature †: grant him his Democracy, and it
exists in his Democracy [f].

---

* See HAWKESWORTH's *Voyages.*

[e] The condition of these imaginary sovereigns puts one in mind
of the story of, I forget what King's Fool. The Fool had stuck
himself up one day, with great gravity, in the King's throne; with
a stick, by way of a sceptre, in one hand, and a ball in the other:
being asked what he was doing? he answered, " *reigning.*" Much
the same sort of reign, I take it, would be that of the members of
our Author's Democracy.

† V. supra, ch. I. par. VI.

[f] What is curious is, that the same persons who tell you
(having read as much) that Democracy is a form of Government
under which the supreme power is vested in all the members of a
state, will also tell you (having also read as much) that the Athenian Common-wealth was a Democracy. Now the truth is, that in

XXXV. The qualification of *goodness*, I think it
was, that belonged to the Government of *all*, while
there was such a Government. This having taken
its flight, as we have seen, to the region of non-
entities, the qualification that was designed for it
remains upon his hands: he is at liberty, therefore,
to make a compliment of it to Aristocracy or to
Monarchy, which best suits him. Perhaps it were
as well to give it to Monarchy; the title of that
form of government to its own peculiar qualification,
power, being, as we have seen, rather an equivocal
one: or else, which, perhaps, is as good a way of
settling matters as any, he may set them to cast
lots.

CHAP. II.

The qualifica-
tion designed
for it become
vacant.

the Athenian Common-wealth, upon the most moderate computation, it is not one tenth part of the inhabitants of the Athenian
state that ever at a time partook of the supreme power: women,
children, and slaves, being taken into the account[*]. Civil Lawyers, indeed, will tell you, with a grave face, that a slave is *nobody;*
as Common Lawyers will, that a bastard is the *son of nobody.* But,
to an unprejudiced eye, the condition of a state is the condition of
all the individuals, without distinction, that compose it.

[*] See, among Mr. HUME's *Essays,* that *on the populousness of
ancient nations.*

CHAP. III.

BRITISH CONSTITUTION.

CHAP. III.

Our Author's panegyric on the British Constitution.

I. With a set of *data*, such as we have seen in the last chapter, we may judge whether our Author can meet with any difficulty in proving the British Constitution to be the best of all possible governments, or indeed any thing else that he has a mind. In his paragraph on this subject there are several things that lay claim to our attention. But it is necessary we should have it under our eye.

The paragraph recited.

II. " But happily for us in this island the British " Constitution has long remained, and I trust will " long continue, a standing exception to the truth " of this observation. For, as with us the executive " power of the laws is lodged in a single person, " they have all the advantages of strength and dis- " patch that are to be found in the most absolute " monarchy; and, as the legislature of the kingdom " is entrusted to three distinct powers entirely in- " dependent of each other; first, the King; se- " cond, the Lords Spiritual and Temporal, which " is an aristocratical assembly of persons selected " for their piety, their birth, their wisdom, their

" valour or their property; and third, the House CHAP. III.
" of Commons, freely chosen by the people from
" among themselves, which makes it a kind of de-
" mocracy; as this aggregate body, actuated by
" different springs, and attentive to different inte-
" rests, composes the British Parliament, and has
" the supreme disposal of every thing; there can no
" inconvenience be attempted by either of the three
" branches, but will be withstood by one of the
" other two; each branch being armed with a
" negative power sufficient to repel any innovation
" which it shall think inexpedient or dangerous."

III. " Here then is lodged the sovereignty of the —And that
" British Constitution; and lodged as beneficially it. which follows
" as is possible for society. For in no other shape
" could we be so certain of finding the three great
" qualities of Government so well and so happily
" united. If the supreme power were lodged in
" any one of the three branches separately, we must
" be exposed to the inconveniencies of either abso-
" lute monarchy, aristocracy, or democracy; and
" so want two of the principal ingredients of good
" polity, either virtue, wisdom, or power. If it were
" lodged in any two of the branches; for instance,
" in the King and House of Lords, our laws might
" be providentally made and well executed, but they
" might not always have the good of the people, in
" view: if lodged in the King and Commons, we

CHAP. III. " should want that circumspection and mediatory
" caution, which the wisdom of the Peers is to
" afford: if the supreme rights of legislature were
" lodged in the two Houses only, and the King had
" no negative upon their proceedings, they might
" be tempted to encroach upon the royal preroga-
" tive, or perhaps to abolish the kingly office, and
" thereby weaken (if not totally destroy) the strength
" of the executive power. But the constitutional
" government of this island is so admirably temper-
" ed and compounded, that nothing can endanger
" or hurt it, but destroying the equilibrium of power
" between one branch of the legislature and the rest.
" For if ever it should happen that the independence
" of any one of the three should be lost, or that it
" should become subservient to the views of either
" of the other two, there would soon be an end
" of our constitution.   The legislature would be
" changed from that which was originally set up by
" the general consent and fundamental act of the
" society; and such a change, however affected, is,
" according to Mr. Locke (who perhaps carries his
" theory too far) at once an entire dissolution of the
" bands of Government, and the people would be
" reduced to a state of anarchy, with liberty to con-
" stitute to themselves a new legislative power."

Executive
power--the
mention of

IV. In considering the first of these two paragraphs, in the first place, a phenomenon we should

little expect to see from any thing that goes before, CHAP. III.
is a certain *executive power*, that now, for the first
time, bolts out upon us without warning or introduction.

It—Incongru-
ously intro-
duced.

The power, the only power our Author has been
speaking of all along till now, is the *legislative*.
'Tis to this, and this alone, that he has given the
name of "*sovereign power*." 'Tis this power, the
different distributions of which he makes the cha-
racteristics of his three different forms of government. 'Tis with these different distributions, distributions made of the legislative power, that,
according to his account, are connected the several
qualifications laid down by him, as " requisites for
" supremacy:" qualifications in the possession of
which consist all the advantages which can belong
to any form of Government. Coming now then
to the British Constitution, it is in the superior
degree in which these qualifications of the legislative body are possessed by it, that its peculiar excellence is to consist. It is by possessing the qualification of strength, that it possesses the advantage
of a monarchy. But how is it then that, by his account, it possesses the qualification of strength? By
any disposition made of the legislative power? By
the legislative power's being lodged in the hands of
a single person, as in the case of a monarchy? No;
but to a disposition made of a new power, which
comes in, as it were, in a parenthesis, a new power

which we now hear of for the first time, a power which has not, by any description given of it, been extinguished from the legislative, an *executive*.

Difficulty of determining what it is as contra-distinct to legislative.

V. What then is this same executive power? I doubt our Author would not find it a very easy matter to inform us. " Why not?" says an objector—" is it not that power which in this country " the King has in addition to his share in the legis- " lative." Be it so: the difficulty for a moment is staved off. But that it is far enough from being solved, a few questions will soon shew us. This power, is it that only which the King really *has*, or is it all that he is said to have? Is it that only which he really has, and which he exercises, or is it that also, which although he be said to have it, he neither does exercise, nor may exercise? Does it include judiciary power or not? If it does, does it include the power of making as well *particular* decisions and orders, as *general, permanent, spontaneous* regulations of procedure, such as are some of those we see made by judges? Doth it include supreme military power, and that as well in ordinary as in a time of martial law? Doth it include the supreme *fiscal* power [a]; and, in general, that power which, extending as well over the public

[a] By *fiscal* power I mean that which in this country is exercised by what is called the Board of Treasury.

money as over every other article of public property, CHAP. III.
may be styled the *dispensatorial* [b]. Doth it include
the power of granting patents for inventions, and
charters of incorporation? Doth it include the
right of making bye-laws in corporations? And is
the right of making bye-laws in corporations the
superior right to that of conferring the power to
make them, or is it that there is an executive
power that is superior to a legislative? This *executive* again, doth it include the right of substitut-
ing the laws of war to the laws of peace; and, *vice
versâ*, the laws of peace to the laws of war? Doth
it include the right of restraining the trade of subjects by treaties with foreign powers? Doth it include the right of delivering over, by virtue of the

[b] By *dispensatorial* power I mean as well that which is exercised by the Board of Treasury, as those others which are executed in the several offices styled with us the War Office, Ad-
miralty Board, Navy Board, Board of Ordnance, and Board of
Works: excepting from the business of all these offices, the power
of appointing persons to fill other subordinate offices: a power
which seems to be of a distinct nature from that of making disposition of any article of public property.

Power, political power, is either over *persons* or over *things*.
The powers, then, that have been mentioned above, in as far as
they concern *things*, are powers over such *things* as are the property of the public: powers which differ in this from those which
constitute private ownership, in that the former are, in the main,
not *beneficial* (that is, to the possessors themselves) and *indiscrimi-
nate*; but *fiduciary*, and *limited* in their exercise to such *acts* as
are conducive to the *special* purposes of *public* benefit and security.

CHAP. III. like treaties, large bodies of subjects to foreign laws?—He that would understand what power is executive and not legislative, and what legislative . and not executive, he that would mark out and delineate the different species of constitutional powers, he that would describe either what *is*, or what *ought to be* the constitution of a country, and particularly of this country, let him *think of these things*.

Independence inaccurately attributed to the three branches of the Government. VI. In the next place we are told in a parenthesis (it being a matter so plain as to be taken for granted) that " each of these branches af the Legislature " is *independent*,"—yes, " *entirely* independent," of the two others.—Is this then really the case? Those who consider the influence which the King and so many of the Lords have in the election of members of the House of Commons; the power which the King has, at a minute's warning, of putting an end to the existence of any House of Commons; those who consider the influence which the King has over both Houses, by offices of dignity and profit given and taken away again at pleasure; those who consider that the King, on the other hand, depends for his daily bread on both Houses, but more particularly on the House of Commons; not to mention a variety of other circumstances that might be noticed in the same view, will judge what degree of precision there was in our Author's meaning, when he so roundly asserted the affirmative.

VII. One parenthesis more: for this sentence CHAP. III.
teems with parenthesis within parenthesis. To this
we are indebted for a very interesting piece of in- A happy dis-
telligence: nothing less than a full and true account station.
of the personal merits of the members of the House
of Lords for the time being. This he is enabled to
do, by means of a contrivance of his own, no less
simple than it is ingenious: to wit, that of looking
at their titles. It is by looking at men's titles that
he perceives, not merely that they *ought* to possess
certain merits, not that there is reason to *wish* they
may possess them, but that they do *actually* possess
them, and that it is by possessing those merits that
they come to possess these titles. Seeing that some
are bishops, he knows that they are pious: seeing
that some are peers, he knows that they are wise,
rich, valiant [c].

[c] " The Lords spiritual and temporal, [p. 50.] which," says
our Author, " *is* an aristocratical assembly of persons selected for
" their piety, their birth, their wisdom, their valour, or their pro-
" perty"—I have distributed, I think, these endowments, as our
Author could not but intend they should be distributed. Birth,
to such of the members of that assembly as have their seat in it by
descent: and, as to those who may chance from time to time to sit
there by *creation*, wisdom, valour, and property in *common* among
the temporal peers; and piety, singly but entirely, among my
Lords the Bishops. As to the other three endowments, if there
were any of them to which these right reverend persons could lay
any decent claim, it would be wisdom: but since worldly wisdom
is what it would be an ill compliment to attribute to them, and

CHAP. III.

Supposed
qualities of
the three pre-
tended forms
of Govern-
ment not ap-
plicable to
our own.

VIII. The more we consider the application he makes of the common-place notions concerning the three forms of Government to our own, the more we shall see the wide difference there is between reading and reflecting. Our own he finds to be a combination of these three. It has a Monarchical branch, an Aristocratical, and a Democratical. The

the wisdom which is from above is fairly included under piety, I conclude that, when secured in the exclusive possession of this grand virtue, they have all that was intended them. There is a remarkable period in our history, at which, measuring by our Author's scale, these three virtues seem to have been at the boiling point. It was in Queen Ann's reign, not long after the time of the hard frost. I mean in the year 1711. In that auspicious year, these three virtues issued forth, it seems, with such exuberance, as to furnish merit enough to stock no fewer than a dozen respectable persons, who, upon the strength of it, were all made Barons in a day. Unhappily indeed, so little read was a right reverend and cotemporary historian*, in our Author's method of " discerning of spirits," as to fancy, it was neither more nor less than the necessity of making a majority that introduced so large a body of new members thus suddenly into the house. But I leave it to those who are read in the history of that time, to judge of the ground there can be for so romantic an imagination. As to piety, the peculiar endowment of the mitre, the stock there is of that virtue, should, to judge by the like standard, be, at all times, pretty much upon a level; at all times, without question, at a *maximum*. This is what we can make the less doubt of, since, with regard to ecclesiastical matters, in general, our Author, as in another place he assures us has had the happiness to find, that "every thing is as it should be†."

* See Bishop Burnet's History of his own Times. Vol. 2.
† Vol. 4. Chap. IV. p. 49.

Aristocratical is the House of Lords; the Democratical is the House of Commons. Much had our
Author read, at school, doubtless, and at college,
of the wisdom and gravity of the Spartan senate:
something, probably, in Montesquieu, and elsewhere, about the Venetian. He had read of the
turbulence and extravagance of the Athenian mob.
Full of these ideas, the House of Lords were to be
our Spartans or Venetians; the House of Commons, our Athenians. With respect then to the
point of wisdom, (for that of honesty we will pass
by) the consequence is obvious. The House of
Commons, however excellent in point of honesty, is
an assembly of less *wisdom* than that of the House
of Lords. This is what our Author makes no scru-
ple of assuring us. A Duke's son gets a seat in
the House of Commons. There needs no more to
make him the very model of an Athenian cobbler.

IX. Let us find out if we can, whence this no- Wisdom, why likely to be
tion of the want of wisdom in the members of a De- *wanting* in the members
mocracy, and of the abundance of it in those of an of a Demo-cracy—
Aristocracy, could have had its rise. We shall
then see with what degree of propriety such a notion can be transferred to *our* Houses of Lords and
Commons.

In the members of a Democracy in particular,
there is likely to be a want of wisdom—Why? The
greater part being poor, are, when they begin to

CHAP. III. take upon them the management of affairs, uneducated: being uneducated, they are illiterate: being
illiterate, they are ignorant. Ignorant, therefore,
and *unwise*, if that be what is meant by ignorant,
they *begin*. Depending for their daily bread on the
profits of some petty traffic, or the labour of some
manual occupation, they are nailed to the work-
board, or the counter. In the business of Government, it is only by fits and starts that they have
leisure so much as to *act :* they have no leisure to
reflect. Ignorant therefore they *continue.*—But in
what degree is this the case with the members of
our House of Commons ?

*...and present
in those of an
Aristocracy.*
X. On the other hand, the members of an Aristocracy, being few, are rich: either they are members of the Aristocracy, because they are rich; or
they are rich, because they are members of the
Aristocracy. Being rich, they are educated : being
educated, they are learned: being learned, they
are knowing. They are at leisure to *reflect,* as well
as *act.* They may therefore naturally be expected
to become more knowing, that is more wise, as
they persevere. In what degree is this the case
with the members of the House of Lords more than
with those of the House of Commons? The fact is,
as every body sees, that either the members of the
House of Commons are as much at leisure as those
of the House of Lords; or, if occupied in such a

way as tends to give them a more tban ordinary
insight into some particular department of Government. In whom shall we expect to find so much
knowledge of Law as in a professed Lawyer? of
Trade, as in a Merchant?

XI. But hold—Our Author, when he attributes
to the members of an Aristocracy more wisdom
than to those of a Democracy, has a reason of his
own. Let us endeavour to understand it, and then
apply it, as we have applied the others. In Aristocratical bodies, we are to understand there is
more *experience:* at least it is intended by some
body or other there *should be:* which, it seems,
answers the same purpose as if there *was.* " In
" Aristocracies," says our Author, there is more
" wisdom to be found, than in the other frames of
" Government; being composed," continues he,
" or intended to be composed, of the most experi-
" enced citizens*." On this ground then it is,
that we are to take for granted, that the members
of the House of Lords have more wisdom among
them, than those of the House of Commons. It is
this article of *experience* that, being a qualification
possessed by the members of an Aristocratical body,
as such, in a superior degree to that in which it
can be possessed by a democratical body, is to

* P. 50.

CHAP. III. afford us a particular ground for attributing a greater share of wisdom to the members of the upper house, than to those of the lower.

Superiority of "experience" how far a proof of superiority of wisdom.

XII. How it is that a member of an aristocracy, as such, is, of all things, to have attained more *experience* than the member of a democracy, our Author has not told us; nor what it is this experience is to consist of. Is it experience of things *preparatory* to, but different from, the business of governing? This should rather go by the name of *knowledge.* Is it experience of the business itself of governing? Let us see. For the member of the one body, as of the other, there must be a time when he first enters upon this business. They both enter upon it, suppose on the same day. Now then is it on that same day that one is more experienced in it than the other? or is it on that day ten years?

---how far attributable to aristocracies in general.

XIII. Those indeed who recollect what we observed but now *, may answer without hesitation,—on that day ten years. The reason was there given. It is neither more nor less, than that want of leisure which the bulk of the numerous members of a Democracy must necessarily labour under, more than those of an Aristocracy. But of this, what intimation is there to be collected, from any thing that has been suggested by our Author?

* V. supra, par. 9.

XIV. So much with respect to Aristocracies in
general. It happens also by accident, that that
particular branch of our *own* government to which
he has given the name of the Aristocratical,—the
House of Lords,—has actually greater opportuni-
ties of acquiring the qualification of experience,
than that other branch, the House of Commons, to
which he has given the name of the democratical.
But to what is this owing? not to any thing in the
characteristic natures of those two bodies, not to
the one's being Aristocratical, and the other Democratical; but to a circumstance, entirely foreign
and accidental, which we shall see presently. But
let us observe his reasoning. The House of Lords,
he says, is an assembly that behoves to have more
wisdom in it, than the House of Commons. This
is the proposition. Now for the proof. The first
is an Aristocratical assembly; the second a Democratical. An Aristocratical assembly has more experience than a Democratical; and on that account more wisdom. Therefore the House of
Lords, as was to be proved, has more wisdom than
the House of Commons. Now, what the whole of
the argument rests upon, we may observe, is this
fact, that an Aristocratical assembly, as such, has
more experience than a Democratical one; but
this, with Aristocratical assemblies in general, we
see, is not, for any reason that our Author has
given us, the case. At the same time with respect

CHAP. III. to our House of Lords in particular, in comparison with the House of Commons, it does happen to be the case, owing to this simple circumstance: the members of the House of Lords, when once they begin to sit, sit on for life: those of the House of Commons only from seven years to seven years, or it may happen, less.

What is to be understood by the word "*experience*."

XV. In speaking, however, in this place, of experience, I would rather be understood to mean opportunity of acquiring experience, than experience itself. For actual experience depends upon other concurrent causes.

Opportunity of experience not the sole cause of wisdom.

XVI. It is, however, from superiority of experience alone, that our Author derives superiority of wisdom. He has, indeed, the proverb in his favour: " Experience," it has been said of old, " is " the Mother of Wisdom :" be it so ;—but then Interest is the Father. There is even an Interest that is the Father of Experience. Among the members of the House of Commons, though none so poor as to be illiterate, are many whose fortunes, according to the common phrase, are yet to make. The fortunes of those of the House of Lords (I speak in general) are made already. The members of the House of Commons may hope to be members of the House of Lords. The members of the House of Lords have no higher House of Lords

to rise to. Is it natural for those to be most active CHAP. III.
who have the *least*, or those who have the *most* interest to be so? Are the experienced those who are
the least, or those who are the most active? Does
experience come to men when asleep, or when
awake? Is it the members of the House of Lords
that are the most active, or of the House of Commons? To speak plain, is it in the House of Lords
that there is most business done, or in the House
of Commons? Was it *after* the *fish* was caught that
the successor of St. Peter used the *net*, or was it
before [i] ? In a word, is there most wisdom ordi-
narily where there is least, or where there is most to
gain by being wise [k]?

[i] Every body has heard the story of him who, from a fisher-
man, was made Archbishop, and then Pope. While Archbishop,
it was his custom every day, after dinner, to have a fishing net
spread upon his table, by way of a memento, as he used to say, of
the meanness of his original. This farcical ostentation of humility
was what, in those days, contributed not a little to the encrease of
his reputation. Soon after his exaltation to St. Peter's chair,
one of his intimates was taking notice to him, one day, when dinner was over, of the table's not being decked as usual. " Peace,"
answered the Holy Father, " when the fish is caught, there is no
" occasion for the net."

[k] In the House of Commons itself, is it by the opulent and independent Country gentlemen that the chief business of the House
is transacted, or by aspiring, and perhaps needy Courtiers? The
man who would persevere in the toil of Government, without any
other reward than the favour of the people, is certainly the man
for the people to make choice of. But such men are at best but

CHAP. III.   XVII. A word or two more with respect to the

Mediatory caution not the peculiar province of the Lords.

characteristic qualifications, as our Author states them, of the higher assembly of our legislature. Experience is, in virtue of their being an aristocratical assembly, to afford them *wisdom* : thus far we were arrived before. But he now pushes the deduction a step farther.—Wisdom is to afford them " circumspection and mediatory caution:" qualifications which it seems as if we should see nothing of, were it not for them. Let us now put a case. The business,indeed, that originates in the House of Lords is, as things stand, so little, that our Author seems to forget that there is any. However, some there is. A bill then originates with the Lords, and is sent down to the Commons.—As to " circumspection" I say nothing : *that*, let us hope, is not wanting to either House. But whose province is " mediatory caution," now ?

The Democratical branch of our Legislature, upon our Author's principles, not distinguishable from the Aristocratical.

XVIII. Thus much concerning these two branches of our legislature, so long as they continue what, according to our Author's principles, they are at present: the House of Lords the Aristocratical branch: the House of Commons the Democratical. A little while and we shall see them so ; but again a little while, perhaps, and we shall not see them so. For by what characteristic does our

rare. Were it not for those children of Corruption we have been speaking of, the business of the state, I doubt, would stagnate.

Author distinguish an Aristocratical legislative body from a Democratical one? By that of *number*: by the number of the persons that compose them: by that, and that alone: for no other has he given. Now, therefore, to judge by that, the House of Lords, at present, indeed, *is* the Aristocratical branch: the House of Commons in comparison at least with the other, the Democratical. Thus far is well. But should the list of nobility swell at the rate we have sometimes seen it, there is an assignable period, and that, perhaps, at no very enormous distance, at which the assembly of the Lords will be more numerous than that of the Commons. Which will *then* be the Aristocratical branch of our Legislature? Upon our Author's principles, the House of Commons. Which the Democratical? The House of Lords.

CHAP. III.

XIX. The final cause we are to observe, and finishing exploit, the " *portus et sabbatum*," as Lord Bacon might perhaps have called it [*l*], of this sublime and edifying dissertation, is this demonstration, he has been giving us, of the perfection of the British Form of Government. This demonstration (for by no less a title ought it to be called) is founded, we may have observed, altogether upon

All-perfection of the British Constitution mathematically demonstrated.

[*l*] It is what he says of Theology with respect to the Sciences. —V. Augm. Scient. L. VIII. c. III. p. 97.

CHAP.III. the properties of *numbers :* properties, newly discovered indeed, and of an extraordinary complection, *moral* properties; but properties, however, so it seems, of numbers *. 'Tis in the nature then of numbers we shall find these characteristic properties of the three Forms of Government, if any where. Now the properties of numbers are universally allowed to be the proper subject of that mode of demonstration which is called *mathematical.* The proof our Author has given has therefore already in it the *essence* of such a demonstration. To be complete at all points, it wants nothing but the *form.* This deficiency is no other than what an under-rate workman might easily supply. A mere technical operation does the business. That humble task it shall be my endeavour to perform. The substantial honour I ascribe wholly to our Author, to whom only it is most due.

The demonstration drawn up in form.

XX. PROPOSITION. *Theorem.*—The British Government is all-perfect.

DEMONSTRATION.

| By definition, | 1 | The British Government = Monarchy + Aristocracy + Democracy. |
| Again, by definition, | 2 | Monarchy = the Government of 1. |

* V. supra.

Also,	3	Democracy = the Government CHAP. III. of *all*.
Also,	4	Aristocracy = the Government of some number between 1 and *all*.
Put	5	*All* = 1,000,000.
Put also	6	The number of governors in an Aristocracy = 1,000.
Now then, by assumption,	7	1 has + strength —wisdom — honesty.
Also,	8	1,000 has + wisdom—strength —honesty.
Also,	9	1,000,000 has + honesty — strength — wisdom.
Rejecting—wisdom —honesty in [*m*] in [7]	10	1 has + strength.
Also rejecting — strength — honesty in [8]	11	1,000 has + wisdom.
Also rejecting — strength — wisdom in [9]	12	1,000,000 has + honesty.

The demon-stration drawn up in form.

[*m*] Which is done without any sort of ceremony, the quantities marked in this step with the negative sign, being as so many *fluents*, which are at a *maximum*, or a *minimum*, just as happens to be most convenient.

CHAP. III.

The demonstration drawn up in form.

Putting toge-ther the ex-pressions [10], [11], and [12],	13	1 + 1,000, + 1,000,000 has strength + wisdom + ho-nesty.
But by the de-finitions [1], [2], [3], [4], and the sup-positions [5], [6],	14	The British Government = 1 + 1,000 + 1,000,000.
Therefore, by [13]	15	The British Government has + strength + wisdom + honesty.
Changing the expression,	16	The British Government is all-powerful + all-wise + all-honest.
But by defini-tion	17	All-powerful + all-wise + all-honest = all-perfect.
Therefore, by [16], and [17]	18	The British Government is all-perfect. Q. E. D.

₊ SCHOLIUM. After the same manner it may be proved to be *all-weak, all-foolish,* and *all-knavish.*

Conclusion of the Chapter.

XXI. Thus much for the British Constitution; and for the grounds of that pre-eminence which it boasts, I trust, indeed, not without reason, above

all others that are known : Such is the idea our CHAP. III.
Author gives us of those grounds.—" You are not
" satisfied with it then," says some one.—Not per- Conclusion of the Chapter.
fectly.—" What is then your own ?"—In truth this
is more than I have yet quite settled. I may have
settled it with myself, and not think it worth the
giving : but if ever I do think it worth the giving,
it will hardly be in the form of a comment on a digression stuffed into the belly of a definition. At
any rate it is not likely to be much wished for, by
those, who have read what has been given us on
this subject by an ingenious foreigner : since it is to
a foreigner we were destined to owe the best idea
that has yet been given of a subject so much our
own. Our Author has copied : but Mr. de L'OLME
has thought.

The topic which our Author has thus brought
upon the carpet (let any one judge with what
necessity) is in respect to some parts of it that we
have seen, rather of an invidious nature. Since,
however, it *has* been brought upon the carpet, I
have treated it with that plainness with which an
Englishman of all others is bound to treat it, because an Englishman may thus treat it and be safe.
I have said what the subject seemed to demand,
without any fear indeed, but without any wish, to
give offence : resolving not to permit myself to
consider how this or that man might chance to take
it. I have spoken without sycophantical respects

CHAP. III.

Conclusion of the Chapter.

indeed, yet I hope not without decency : certainly without any party spleen. I chose rather to leave it to our Author to compliment men in the lump: and to stand aghast with admiration at the virtues of men unknown*. Our Author will do as shall seem meet to him. For my part, if ever I stand forth and sing the song of eulogy to great men, it shall be not because they *occupy* their station, but because they *deserve* it.

* V. supra, par. 7.

CHAP. IV.

RIGHT OF THE SUPREME POWER TO MAKE
LAWS.

I. WE now come to the third topic touched upon in the digression; namely, the *right*, as our Author phrases it, which the Supreme Power has of making laws. And this topic occupies one pretty long paragraph. The title here given to it is the same which in the next succeeding paragraph he has found for it himself. This is fortunate: for, to have been obliged to find a title for it myself, is what would have been to the last degree distressing. To *intitle* a discourse, is to represent the drift of it. But, to represent the drift of this, is a task which, so long at least as I confine my consideration to the paragraph itself, bids defiance to my utmost efforts.

CHAP. IV.

Subject of the paragraph in question as stated by our Author.

II. 'Tis to another passage or two, a passage or two that we have already seen starting up in distant parts of this digression, that I am indebted for such conjectures as I have been able to make up.

Drift of it as conjectured.

These conjectures, however, I could not have ventured so far to rely on, as on the strength of

CHAP. IV. them to have furnished the paragraph with a title of my own framing. The danger of misrepresentation was too great; a kind of danger which a man cannot but lie imminently exposed to, who ventures to put a precise meaning upon a discourse which in itself has none. That I may just mention, however, in this place, the result of them; what he is really aiming at, I take it, is, to inculcate a persuasion that in every state there must subsist, in some hands 'or other, a power that is *absolute.* I mention it thus prematurely, that the reader may have some clue to guide him in his progress through the paragraph; which is now time I should recite.

The paragraph recited. III. "Having," says our Author, "thus cursorily "considered the three usual species of government, "and our own singular constitution, selected and "compounded from them all, I proceed to observe, "that, as the power of making laws constitutes the "supreme authority, so wherever the supreme au- "thority in any state resides, it is the right of that "authority to make laws; that is, in the words of "our definition, to prescribe the rule of civil action. "And this may be discovered from the very end "and institution of civil states. For a state is a "collective body, composed of a multitude of indi- "viduals united for their safety and convenience, "and intended to act together as one man. If it "therefore is to act as one man, it ought to act by

" one uniform will. But in as much as political CHAP. IV.
" communities are made up of many natural per-
" sons, each of whom has his particular will and in-
" clination, these several wills cannot by any *natural*
" union be joined together, or tempered and dis-
" posed into a lasting harmony, so as to constitute
" and produce that one uniform will of the whole.
" It can therefore be no otherwise produced than by
" a *political* union; by the consent of all persons to
" submit their own private wills to the will of one
" man, or of one, or more assemblies of men, to
" whom the supreme authority is entrusted: and
" this will of that one man, or assemblage of men is,
" in different states, according to their different
" constitutions, understood to be law."

IV. The other passages which suggested to me *The sense of it considered in itself.*
the construction I have ventured to put upon this,
shall be mentioned by and by. First, let us try
what is to be made of it by itself.

V. The obscurity in which the first sentence of *The leading argument is nugatory.*
this paragraph is enveloped, is such, that I know
not how to go about bringing it to light, without
borrowing a word or two of logicians. Laying aside
the preamble, the body of it, viz. " *as* the power of
" making laws constitutes the supreme authority, so
" wherever the supreme authority in any state
" resides, it is the right of that authority to make

CHAP. IV. "laws," may be considered as constituting that sort of syllogism which logicians call an *enthymem*. An *enthymem* consists of two *propositions*; a *consequent* and an *antecedent*. " The power of making laws," says our Author, " constitutes the supreme autho- " rity." This is his antecedent. From hence it is he concludes, that " wherever the supreme authority " in any state resides, it is the right of that au- " thority to make laws." This then is his *conse-quent.*

Now so it is, that this *antecedent*, and this *conse-quent*, for any difference at least that I can possibly perceive in them, would turn out, were they but correctly worded, to mean precisely the same thing : for, after saying that " the power of making laws " constitutes the supreme authority," to tell us that, for that reason, " the supreme authority" is (or has) the power (or the right) of making laws, is given us, I take it, much the same sort of information, as it would be to us to be told that a thing is so, *because* it is so : a sort of truth which there seems to be no very great occasion to send us upon " discovering, " in the end and institution of civil states." That by the " sovereign power," he meant " the power of " making laws ;" this, or something like it, is no more indeed than what he had told us over and over, and over again, with singular energy and anxiety, in his 46th page, in his 49th, and in, I know not how many, pages besides : always taking care, for pre-

cision's sake, to give a little variety to the expres-   CHAP.IV.
sion: the words *"power"* and *"authority*," sometimes, seemingly put for the same idea ; sometimes
seemingly opposed to each other : both of them
sometimes denoting the *fictitious* being, the *abstract
quality ;* sometimes the *real* being or beings, the
person or *persons* supposed to *possess* that *quality.—*
Let us disentangle the sense from these ambiguities ;
let us learn to speak distinctly of the *persons,* and
of the *quality* we attribute to them; and then let
us make another effort to find a meaning for this
perplexing passage.

VI. By the " supreme authority" then, (we may The antece-
                                                dent stated
suppose our Author to say) " I mean the same anew.
" thing as when I say the power of making laws."
This is the proposition we took notice of above,
under the name of the *antecedent.* This antecedent
then, we may observe, is a definition: a definition,
to wit, of the phrase " supreme authority." Now to
define a phrase is, to translate it into another
phrase, suppose to be better understood, and expressive of the same ideas. The supposition here
then is, that the reader was already, of himself,
tolerably well acquainted with the import of the
phrase " power of making laws ;" that he was not
at all, or was however less acquainted with the
import of the phrase " supreme authority." Upon
this supposition then, it is, that in order to his being

H

CHAP. IV. made clearly to understand the latter, he is informed of its being synonymous to the former. Let us now introduce the mention of the *person :* let us add the word "*person*" to the definition; it will be the same definition still in substance, only a little more fully and precisely worded. *For a person to possess* the supreme authority, is *for a person to possess* the power of making laws. This then is what in substance has been already laid down in the *antecedent*.

The consequent new stated. VII. Now let us consider the *consequent ;* which, when detached from the context, may be spoken of as making a sentence of itself. " Wherever," says he, " the supreme authority in any state resides, it " is the *right* of that authority to make Laws."—By "*wherever*" I take it for granted, he means, " *in* "*whatever persons :*" by " *authority*," in the former part of the sentence,—*power ;* by the same word, "*authority*," in the latter part of the sentence,— *persons*. Corrected therefore, the sentence will stand thus : *In whatever persons in any state the supreme power resides, it is the right of those persons to make Laws.*

That it is identical with the antecedent. VIII. The only word now remaining undisposed of, is the word " *right.*" And what to think of this, I must confess I know not : whether our Author had a meaning in it, or whether he had none. It is inserted, we may observe, in the latter part only

of the sentence: it appears not in the former. CHAP.IV.
Concerning this omission, two conjectures here
present themselves: it may have happened by accident; or it may have been made by design. If by
accident, then the case is, that the idea annexed
to the word "*right*" is no other than what was
meant to be included in the former part of the sentence, in which it is *not* expressed; as well as in the
latter, in which it *is*. In this case it may, without
any change in the signification, be expressed in both.
Let it then be expressed, and the sentence, take it
all together, will stand thus: *In whatever persons*
the right of exercising *supreme power in any state*
resides, it is the right *of those persons to make Laws.*
If this conjecture be the true one, and I am apt to
think it is, we see once more, and, I trust, beyond
all doubt, that the *consequent* in this *enthymem* is but
a repetition of the *antecedent*. We may judge then,
whether it is from any such consideration as that of
" the end and institution of civil states," or any
other consideration that we are likely to gain any
further conviction of the truth of this *conclusion,*
than it presents us of itself. We may also form
some judgment before-hand, what use or meaning
there is likely to be in the assemblage of words that
is to follow.

IX. What is possible, notwithstanding, however —or else
nothing to the
improbable, is, that the omission we have been purpose.

CHAP.I V speaking of was *designed*. In this case, what we are to understand is, that the word "*right*" *was* meant to introduce a new idea into this latter part of the sentence, over and above any that was meant to be suggested by the former. "*Right*" then, according to this construction, in the one place, is to be considered as put in contradistinction to *fact* in the other. The sense is then, that *whatever persons* do actually *exercise supreme power*, (or what, according to the *antecedent* of the *enthymem*, is the same thing, *the power of making laws*) *those persons* have the right to *exercise it*. But, in this case, neither does what is given as a *consequence* in any respect follow from the *antecedent*, nor can *any thing be* made of it, but what is altogether foreign to the rest of the discourse. So much indeed, that it seems more consonant to probability, as well as more favourable to our Author, to conclude that he had no meaning at all, than that he had this.

The rest of the paragraph new stated— supposed drift of it. X. Let us now try what we can make of the remainder of the paragraph. Being usher'd in by the word "*for*," it seems to lay claim to the appellation of an argument. This argument setting out, as we have seen, without an object, seems however to have found something like one at last, as if it had picked it up by the way. This object, if I mistake it not, is to persuade men, that the *supreme power*, (that is the *person* or *persons* in use to exercise the supreme power in a state) ought, in all points, without exception, to be obeyed. What men intend, he says, to do when they are in a state, is to act, as if they were but "one man." But one man has but one will belonging to him. What they intend therefore, or what they *ought* to intend, (a slight difference which our Author seems not to be well aware of) is, to act as if they had but one will. To act as if they had but one will, the way is, for them to "join" all their wills "together." To do this, the most obvious way would be to join them "*naturally:*" but, as *wills* will not splice and dovetail like deal boards, the only feasible way is to join them "*politically.*" Now the only way for men to join their wills together *politically*, is for them all to consent to submit their wills to the will of one. This one will, to which all others are to be submitted, is the will of those persons wh o are in use to exercise the supreme power; whose wills again, when there happens to be many of them, have, by a process of which our Author has said nothing, been reduced (as we must suppose) into *one* already. So far our Author's argument. The above is the substance of it fairly given; not altogether with so much ornament, indeed, as he has given it, but, I trust, with somewhat more precision. The whole concludes, we may observe, with our Author's favourite identical proposition, or something like it, now for the twentieth time repeated.

CHAP. IV.

The rest of the paragraph new stated.

CHAP. IV.   XI. Taking it altogether, it is, without question,

Weakness of
it as a persoa-
sive to obedi-
ence.
a very ingenious argument: nor can any thing in
the world answer the purpose better, except just in
the case where it happens to be wanted.   Not but
that a veteran antagonist, trained up in the regular
and accustomed discipline of legal fencing, such an
one, indeed, *might* contrive perhaps, with due management, to give our Author the honour of the field.
But should some undisciplined blunderer, like the
Commissary's landlady, thrust in *quart*, when he
should have thrust in *tierce*, I doubt much whether
he might not get within our Author's *guard*.—I
" intend ?"—I " consent ?"—I " submit" myself?
—' Who are you, I wonder, that should know what
' I do better than I do myself? As to " *submitting*
' "*my will*" to the wills of the people who made
' this law you are speaking of,—what I know is,
' that I never " intended" any such thing : I abo-
' minate them, I tell you, and all they ever did, and
' have always *said* so : and as to my " consent," so
' far have I been from giving it to their law, that,
' from the first to the last, I have protested against
' it with all my might.' So much for our refractory
disputant.—What I should say to him I know : but
what our Author could find to say in answer to him,
is more than I can imagine [*b*].

[*b*] One thing in the paragraph we are considering is observ-
able ; it is the concluding sentence, in which he brings together the

XII. Let us now return and pick up those other CHAP. IV.
passages which we supposed to have a respect to A prior para-
the same design that seems to be in view in this. posed to be
First comes the short introductory paragraph that object of this.
ushers in the whole digression: a paragraph which,
however short, and however imperfect with respect
to the purpose of giving a general view of the contents of those which follow it, was, in despite of
method, to expatiate upon this subject.   Upon this
subject, indeed, he does expatiate with a force of
argument and energy of expression which nothing
can withstand.   " This," it begins, " will neces-
" sarily lead us into a short enquiry concerning the
" nature of society and civil government*."—This
is all the intimation it gives of the contents of those
paragraphs we have examined.   Upon *this* before
us it touches in energetic terms ; but more energetic

ideas of *law* and *will.* Here then, in the tail of a digression, he
comes nearer in fact, though without being aware of it, to the
giving a just and precise idea of a law, than in any part of the
definition itself from whence he is digressing. If, instead of saying
that a law is a *will,* he had called it the *expression* of a *will,* and
that sort of expression of a will which goes by the name of a *command,* his definition would, so far as this goes, have been clear as
well as right. As it is, it is neither the one nor the other. But of
this more, if at all, in another place. The definition of law is a
matter of too much nicety and importance to be dispatched in a
note.

* 1 Comm. 47.

CHAP. IV. than precise.—" And the *natural*" (it continues)
" and *inherent* right that belongs to the sovereignty
" of a state," (*natural* right, observe, that belongs
to the sovereignty of a *political* society) " wherever
" that sovereignty be lodged, of making and en-
" forcing laws."

Another.

XIII. This is not all. The most emphatical passage is yet behind. It is a passage in that short
paragraph * which we found to contain such a variety of matter. He is there speaking of the several
forms of government now in being. "However
" they began," says he, " or by what right soever
" they subsist, there *is* and *must be* in all of them a
" *supreme, irresistable, absolute, uncontrouled* autho-
" rity, in which the *jura summi imperii*, or the rights
" of sovereignty reside."

Agitation he
betrays.

XIV. The vehemence, the δεινοτης, of this passage
is remarkable. He ransacks the language: he piles
up, one upon another, four of the most tremendous
epithets he can find; he heaps **Ossa** upon **Pelion**:
and, as if the English tongue did not furnish expressions strong or imposing enough, he tops the
whole with a piece of formidable Latinity. From
all this agitation, it is plain, I think, there is a something which he has very much at heart; which he

---

* 1 Comm. p. 48, supra ch. II. par. 11.

wishes, but fears, perhaps, to bring out undisguised; CHAP. IV.
which in several places, notwithstanding, bursts out
involuntarily, as it were, before he is well ready for
it; and which, a certain discretion, getting at last the
upper hand of propensity, forces, as we have seen,
to dribble away in a string of obscure sophisms.
Thus oddly enough it happens, that that passage of
them all, which, if I mistake not, is the only one that
was meant to be dedicated expressly to the subject,
is the least explicit on it [c].

XV. A courage much stauncher than our Author's Cause of it.
might have wavered here. A task of no less intricacy was here to be travelled through, than that
of adjusting the claims of those two jealous antago-
nists, Liberty and Government. A more invidious
ground is scarcely to be found any where within the
field of politics. Enemies encompass the traveller
on every side. He can scarce stir but he must expect to be assaulted with the war-hoop of political
heresy from one quarter or another. Difficult
enough is the situation of him, who, in these defiles,
feels himself impelled one way by fear, and another
by affection.

[c] Another passage or two there is which might seem to glance
the same way: but these I pass over as less material, after those
which we have seen.

CHAP. IV.

Resource he finds in obscurity.

XVI. To return to the paragraph which it was the more immediate business of this chapter to examine:—Were the path of obscurity less familiar to our Author, one should be tempted to imagine he had struck into it on the particular occasion before us, in the view of extricating himself from this dilemma. A discourse thus prudently indeterminate might express enough to keep fair with the rulers of the earth, without setting itself in direct array against the prejudices of the people. Viewed by different persons, it might present different aspects: to men in power it might recommend itself, and that from the first, under the character of a practical lesson of obedience for the use of the people ; while among the people themselves it might pass muster, for a time at least, in quality of a string of abstract scientific propositions of jurisprudence. It is not till some occasion for making application of it should occur, that its true use and efficacy would be brought to light. The people, no matter on what occasion, begin to murmur, and concert measures of resistance. Now then is the time for the latent virtues of this passage to be called forth. The book is to be opened to them, and in this passage they are to be shewn, what of themselves, perhaps, they would never have observed, a set of arguments curiously strung together and wrapped up, in proof of the universal expedience, or rather *necessity*, of submission : a necessity which is to arise, not out

of the reflection that *the probable mischiefs of resist-* CHAP. IV.
ance are greater than the probable mischiefs of obe-
dience; not out of any such debateable considera- Resource he
finds in ob-·
tion; but out of a something that is to be much scurity.
more cogent and effectual: to wit, a certain *meta-*
physico-legal impotence, which is to beget in them
the sentiment, and answer all the purposes of a
natural one. Armed, and full of indignation, our
malecontents are making their way to the royal
palace. In vain. A certain *estoppel* being made
to bolt out upon them, in the manner we have seen,
by the force of our Author's legal engineering, their
arms are to fall, as it were by enchantment, from
their hands. To disagree, to clamour, to oppose,
to take back, in short, their wills again, is now,
they are told, too late: it is what *cannot* be done:
their wills have been put in *hotchpot* along with
the rest: they *have* " united,"—they *have* " con-
sented,"—they *have* " *sub*mitted."— Our Author
having thus *put his hook into their nose,* they are to
go back as they came, and all is peace. An ingenious contrivance this enough : but popular passion
is not to be fooled, I doubt, so easily. Now and
then, it is true, one error may be driven out, for a
time, by an opposite error: one piece of nonsense
by another piece of nonsense : but for barring the
door effectually and for ever against all error and
all nonsense, there is nothing like the simple truth.

CHAP. IV.

Inconsis-
tency of the
present pas-
sage with a
former.
XVII. After all these pains taken to inculcate unreserved submission, would any one have expected to see our Author himself among the most eager to excite men to disobedience? and that, perhaps, upon the most frivolous pretences? in short, upon any pretence whatsoever? Such, however, upon looking back a little, we shall find him. I say, among the most eager; for other men, at least the most enlightened advocates for liberty, are content with leaving it to subjects to resist, for their own sakes, on the footing of *permission:* this will not content our Author, but he must be forcing it upon them as a point of *duty.*

XVIII. 'Tis in a passage antecedent to the digression we are examining, but in the same section, that, speaking of the pretended law of Nature, and of the law of Revelation, "no human laws," he says, "should be *suffered* to contradict these*." The expression is remarkable. It is not that no human laws should contradict them : but that no human laws should be suffered to contradict them. He then proceeds to give us an example. This example, one might think, would be such as should have the effect of softening the dangerous tendency of the rule :—on the contrary, it is such as cannot

* 1 Comm. p. 42.

but enhance it [*d*]; and, in the application of it to CHAP. IV.
the rule, the substance of the latter is again repeated
in still more explicit and energetic terms. " Nay,"
says he, speaking of the act he instances, " if any
" human law should allow or enjoin us to commit
" it, we are BOUND TO TRANSGRESS that human
" law, or else we must offend both the natural and
" the divine."

XIX. The propriety of this dangerous maxim, so Dangerous
far as the Divine Law is concerned, is what I must tendency of it.
refer to a future occasion for more particular consideration [*e*]. As to the LAW *of Nature*, if (as I

[*d*] It is that of murder. In the word here chosen there lurks
a fallacy which makes the proposition the more dangerous as it is
the more plausible. It is too important to be altogether passed
over: at the same time that a slight hint of it, in this place, is all
that can be given. Murder is *killing* under certain *circumstances.*
—Is the human law then to be allowed to define, in *dernier resort,*
what shall be those *circumstances,* or is it not? If yes, the case of
a "human law allowing or enjoining us to commit it," is a case
that is not so much as supposable: if *no,* adieu to all human laws:
to the fire with our Statutes at large, our Reports, our Institutes,
and all that we have hitherto been used to call our law books; our
law books, the only law books we can be safe in trusting to, are
Puffendorf and the Bible.

[*e*] According to our Author, indeed, it should be to no purpose to make any separate mention of the two laws; since the
Divine Law, he tells us, is but "a part of" that of Nature*. Of
consequence, with respect to that part, at least, which is common
to both, to be contrary to the one, is, of course, to be contrary to
the other.   * 1 Comm. p. 42.

CHAP. IV. trust it will appear) it be nothing but a phrase [*f*];

Dangerous if there be no other medium for proving any act to
tendency of it. be an offence against it, than the mischievous tendency of such act; if there be no other medium for
proving a law of the *state* to be contrary to it, than
the *inexpediency* of such law, unless the bare un-
founded disapprobation of any one who thinks of it
be called a proof; if a test for distinguishing such
laws as would be *contrary* to the LAW *of Nature*
from such as, *without* being contrary to it, are
simply *inexpedient,* be that which neither our Author, nor any man else, so much as pretended ever
to give; if, in a word, there be scarce any law
whatever but what those who have not liked it have
found, on some account or another, to be repugnant
to some text of scripture; I see no remedy but that
the natural tendency of such dotrine is to impel a
man, by the force of conscience, to rise up in arms
against any law whatever that he happens not to
like. What sort of government it is that can consist with such a disposition, I must leave to our
Author to inform us.

The principle   XX. It is the principle of *utility,* accurately ap-
of *utility* the
only guide   prehended and steadily applied, that affords the
under these
difficulties.   only clew to guide a man through these streights.
It is for that, if any, and for that alone to furnish a

[*f*] This is what there would be occasion to shew more at large
in examining some former parts of this section.

decision which neither party shall dare in *theory* to CHAP. IV.
disavow.   It is something to reconcile men even in
theory.   They are, at least, *something* nearer to an
effectual union, than when at variance as well in
respect to theory as of practice.

XXI. In speaking of the supposed contract Juncture for
between King and people*, I have already had oc- resistance.
casion to give the description, and, as it appears to
me, the only *general* description that *can* be given,
of that juncture at which, and not before, resistance
to government becomes *commendable*; or, in other
words, reconcilable to just notions, whether of
legal or not, at least of *moral*, and, if there be any
difference, *religious* duty†.   What was there said
was spoken, at the time, with reference to that particular branch of government which was then in
question; the branch that in this country is administered by the King.   But if it was just, as
applied to *that* branch of government, and in *this*
country, it could only be for the same reason that
it is so when applied to the *whole* of government,
and that in *any* country whatsoever.   It is *then*, we
may say, and not till then, allowable to, if not incumbent on, every man, as well on the score of *duty*
as of *interest*, to enter into measures of resistance;
when, according to the best calculation he is able to

* Ch. I.   † See Ch. V. par. 7, note [b].

CHAP.IV. make, *the probable mischiefs of resistance* (speaking
with respect to the community in general) *appear
less to him than the probable mischiefs of submission.*
This then is to him, that is to each man in particular, the *juncture for resistance.*

Not charac-
terizable by
any *common*
sign.

XXII. A natural question here is—by what *sign*
shall this juncture be known? By what *common*
signal alike conspicuous and perceptible to all? A
question which is readily enough started, but to
which, I hope, it will be almost as readily perceived
that it is impossible to find an answer. *Common*
sign for such a purpose, I, for my part, know of
none : he must be more than a prophet, I think, that
can shew us one. For that which shall serve as a
particular sign to each particular person, I have
already given one—his own internal persuasion of
a balance of *utility* on the side of resistance.

Freedom in a
government
depends not
upon any
limitation to
the Supreme
Power.

XXIII. Unless such a sign then, which I think
impossible, can be shewn, the *field*, if one may say
so, of the supreme governor's authority, though not
infinite, must unavoidably, I think, *unless where limited
by express convention* [g], be allowed to be *indefinite.*

[g] This respects the case where one state has, upon *terms*, submitted itself to the government of another : or where the governing bodies of a number of states agree to take directions in certain
specified cases, from some *body* or other that is distinct from all of
them : consisting of members, for instance, appointed out of each.

Nor can I see any narrower, or other bounds to it, CHAP. IV. under this constitution, or under any other yet *freer* constitution, if there be one, than under the most *despotic*. *Before* the juncture I have been describing were arrived, resistance, even in a country like this, would come too soon: were the juncture arrived *already*, the time for resistance would be come already, under such a government even as any one should call *despotic*.

XXIV. In regard to a government that is *free*, and one that is *despotic*, wherein is it then that the difference consists? Is it that those persons in whose hands that power is lodged which is acknowledged to be supreme, have less power in the one than in the other, when it is from custom that they derive it? By no means. It is not that the power of one any more than of the other has any certain bounds to it. The distinction turns upon circumstances of a very different complexion :—on the *manner* in which that whole mass of power, which, taken together, is supreme, is, in a free state, *distributed* among the several ranks of persons that are sharers in it :—on the *source* from whence their titles to it are successively derived :—on the frequent and easy *changes* of condition between govern*ors* and govern*ed*; whereby the interests of the one class are more or less indistinguishably blended with those of the other :—on the *responsibility* of the governors ; or the right

Principal circumstances on which it does depend.

. I

CHAP. IV. which a subject has of having the reasons publicly
assigned and canvassed of every act of power that
is exerted over him :—on the *liberty of the press;* or
the security with which every man, be he of the one
class or the other, may make known his complaints
and remonstrances to the whole community :—on
the *liberty of public association;* or the security with
which malecontents may communicate their sentiments, concert their plans, and practise every mode
of opposition short of actual revolt, before the
executive power can be legally justified in disturbing
them.

Freedom in a
government
how far fa-
vourable to
resistance.

XXV. True then it may be, that, owing to this
last circumstance in particular, in a state thus circumstanced, the road to a revolution, if a revolution
be necessary, is to appearance shorter; certainly
more smooth and easy. More likelihood, certainly
there is of its being such a revolution as shall be
the work of a number; and in which, therefore, the
interests of a number are likely to be consulted.
Grant then, that by reason of these facilitating circumstances, the juncture itself may arrive sooner,
and upon less provocation, under what is called a
free government, than under what is called an
absolute one: grant this;—yet till it *be* arrived
resistance is as much too soon under one of them
as under the other.

XXVI. Let us avow then, in short, steadily but CHAP. IV.
calmly, what our Author hazards with anxiety and
agitation, that the authority of the supreme body
cannot, *unless where limited by express convention*, be
said to have any assignable, any certain bounds.—
That to say there is any act they *cannot* do,—to
speak of any thing of their's as being *illegal*,—as
being *void ;*—to speak of their exceeding their *authority* (whatever be the phrase)—their *power*,—their
right,—is, however common, an abuse of language.

The supreme power not limited in itself.

XXVII. The legislature *cannot* do it? The legislature *cannot* make a law to this effect? Why
cannot? What is there that should hinder them?
Why not *this*, as well as so many other laws mur-
mured at, perhaps, as inexpedient, yet submitted to
without any question of the *right ?* With men of the
same party, with men whose affections are already
listed against the law in question, any thing will go
down : any rubbish is good that will add fuel to the
flame. But with regard to an impartial by-stander,
it is plain that it is not denying the right of the
legislature, their *authority,* their *power*, or whatever
be the word—it is not denying that they *can* do
what is in question—it is not that, I say, or any
discourse verging that way that can tend to give
him the smallest satisfaction.

Arguments that suppose it to be so, un-satisfactory--

XXVIII. Grant even the proposition in general :— *—and inapplic.*

CHAP.IV. What are we the nearer? Grant that there *are* certain
bounds to the *authority* of the legislature:—Of what
use is it to say so, when these bounds are what
nobody has ever attempted to mark out to any
useful purpose; that is, in any such manner whereby
it might be known beforehand what description a
law must be of to fall *within*, and what to fall
beyond them? Grant that there *are* things which
the legislator *cannot* do;—grant that there *are* laws
which exceed the *power* of the legislature to
establish. What rule does this sort of discourse
furnish us for determining whether any one that is
in question is, or is not of the number? As far as I
can discover, none. Either the discourse goes on
in the confusion it began;—either all rests in
vague assertions, and no intelligible argument at all
is offered; or if any, such arguments as are drawn
from the principle of *utility :* arguments which, in
whatever variety of words expressed, come at last to
neither more nor less than this; that the tendency of
the law is, to a greater or a less degree, pernicious.
If this then be the result of the argument, why not
come home to it at once? Why turn aside into a
wilderness of sophistry, when the path of plain
reason is straight before us?

XXIX. What practical inferences those who
maintain this language mean should be deduced
from it, is not altogether clear; nor, perhaps, does

every one mean the same. Some who speak of a CHAP. IV.
law as being *void* (for to this expression, not to travel
through the whole list, I shall confine myself) would
persuade us to look upon the authors of it as having
thereby *forfeited*, as the phrase is, their *whole* power :
as well that of giving force to the particular law in
question, as to any other. These are they who,
had they arrived at the same practical conclusion
through the principle of utility, would have spoken
of the law as being to such a degree pernicious, as
that, were the bulk of the community to see it in its
true light, *the probable mischief of resisting it would
be less than the probable mischief of submitting to it.*
These point, in the first instance, at *hostile* opposition.

XXX. Those who say nothing about forfeiture —or to the judicial power.
are commonly less violent in their views. These are
they who, were they to ground themselves on the
principle of utility, and, to use our language, would
have spoken of the law as being mischievous indeed,
but without speaking of it as being mischievous to
the degree that has been just mentioned. The mode
of opposition which they point to is one which passes
under the appellation of a *legal* one.

XXXI. Admit then the law to be void in their sense, Which tends
to give it a
and mark the consequences. The idea annexed to control over
the legisla-
the epithet *void* is obtained from those instances in tive.

CHAP. IV. which we see it applied to a private instrument. The consequence of a *private* instrument's being void is, that all persons concerned are to act as if no such instrument had existed. The consequence, accordingly, of a *law's* being void must be, that people shall act as if there were no such law about the matter: and therefore that if any person in virtue of the mandate of the law should do any thing in coercion of another person, which without such law he would be punishable for doing, he would still be punishable; to wit, by appointment of the judicial power. Let the law, for instance, be a law imposing a tax: a man who should go about to levy the tax by force would be punishable as a trespasser: should he chance to be killed in the attempt, the person killing him would *not* be punishable as for murder: should he kill, he himself *would*, perhaps, be punishable as for murder. To whose office does it appertain to do those acts in virtue of which such punishment would be inflicted? To that of the Judges. Applied to practice then, the effect of this language is, by an appeal made to the Judges, to confer on those magistrates a controlling power over the acts of the legislature.

---A remedy worse than the disease.

XXXII. By this management a *particular* purpose might, perhaps, by chance be answered: and let this be supposed a good ,one. Still what benefit would, from the *general* tendency of such a doctrine,

and such a practice in conformity to it, accrue to CHAP. IV.
the body of the people is more than I can conceive.
A Parliament, let it be supposed, is too much under
the influence of the Crown : pays too little regard to
the sentiments and the interests of the people. Be
it so.   The people at any rate, if not so great a share
as they might and ought to have, have had, at
least, *some* share in chusing it.   Give to the Judges
a power of annulling its acts ; and you transfer a
portion of the supreme power from an assembly
which the people have had *some* share, at least, in
chusing, to a set of men in the choice of whom they
have not the least imaginable share : to a set of
men appointed solely by the Crown : appointed
solely, and avowedly and *constantly*, by that very
magistrate whose partial and occasional influence
is the very grievance you seek to remedy.

XXXIII. In the heat of debate, some, perhaps, But not so
bad as some
would be for saying of this management that it was might represent it.
transferring at once the supreme authority from the
legislative power to the judicial.   But this would be
going too far on the other side.   There is a wide
difference between a *positive* and a *negative* part in
legislation.   There is a wide difference again between a negative upon *reasons* given, and a
negative without any.   The power of *repeating* a law
even for reasons given is a great power : too great

CHAP. IV. indeed ,for Judges : but still very distinguishable from, and much inferior to that of *making* one [h].

The supreme power limitable by convention.

XXXIV. Let us now go back a little. In denying the existence of any assignable bounds to the supreme power, I added *, " unless where limited by " express convention :" for this exception I could not but subjoin. Our Author indeed, in that passage in which, short as it is, he is the most explicit, leaves, we may observe, no room for it. " How-" ever they began," says he (speaking of the several forms of government) " however they began, " and by what right soever they subsist, there is " and must be in ALL of them an authority that is " absolute...." To say this, however, of *all* governments without exception ;—to say that *no* assemblage of men can subsist in a state of govern-

[h] Notwithstanding what has been said, it would be in vain to dissemble, but that, upon occasion, an appeal of this sort may very well answer, and has, indeed, in general, a tendency to answer, in some sort, the purposes of those who espouse, or profess to espouse, the interests of the people. A public and authorised debate on the propriety of the law is by this means brought on. The artillery of the tongue is played off against the law, under cover of the law itself. An opportunity is gained of impressing sentiments unfavourable to it, upon a numerous and attentive audience. As to any other effects from such an appeal, let us believe that in the instances in which we have seen it made, it is the certainty of miscarriage that has been the encouragement to the attempt.

* V. supra, par. 26.

ment, without being subject to some *one* body whose authority stands unlimited so much as by convention; to say, in short, that not even by convention can any limitation be made to the power of that body in a state which in other respects is supreme, would be saying, I take it, rather too much: it would be saying that there is no such thing as government in the German Empire; nor in the Dutch Provinces; nor in the Swiss Cantons: nor was of old in the Achæan league.

CHAP. IV.

The supreme power limitable by convention.

XXXV. In this mode of limitation I see not what there is that need surprize us. By what is it that any degree of *power* (meaning *political power)* is established? It is neither more nor less, as we have already had occasion to observe *, than a habit of, and disposition to obedience: *habit,* speaking with respect to *past* acts; *disposition,* with respect to *future.* This disposition it is as easy, or I am much mistaken, to conceive as being absent with regard to one sort of acts; as present, with regard to another. For a body then, which is in other respects supreme, to be conceived as being with respect to a certain sort of acts limited, all that is necessary is, that this sort of acts be in its description distinguishable from every other.

—So as the terms of it be explicit.

XXXVI. By means of a convention then we are

Which furnishes what

* V. supra, ch. I. par. 13. note [b].

CHAP. IV.

may be taken for a common signal of resistance.

furnished with that common signal which, in other cases, we despaired of finding *. A certain act is in the instrument of convention specified, with respect to which the government is therein precluded from issuing a law to a certain effect: whether to the effect of commanding the act, of permitting it, or of forbidding it. A law is issued to that effect notwithstanding. The issuing then of such a law (the sense of it, and likewise the sense of that part of the convention which provides against it being supposed clear) is a fact notorious and visible to all: in the issuing then of such a law we have a fact which is *capable* of being taken for that common signal we have been speaking of. These bounds the supreme body in question has marked out to its authority: of such a demarcation then what is the effect? either none at all, or this: that the disposition to obedience confines itself within these bounds. Beyond them the disposition is stopped from extending: beyond them the subject is no more prepared to obey the governing body of his own state, than that of any other. What difficulty, I say, there should be in conceiving a state of things to subsist in which the supreme authority is thus limited,—what greater difficulty in conceiving it with this limitation, than without any, I cannot see. The two states are, I must confess, to me alike conceivable: whether alike expedient,—alike

---

* V. supra, par. 22.

conducive to the happiness of the people, is an- CHAP. IV.
other question.

XXXVII. God forbid, that from any thing here A salvo for
reformation.
said it should be concluded that in any society any
convention is or can be made, which shall have the
effect of setting up an insuperable bar to that which
the parties affected shall deem a reformation :—
God forbid that any disease in the constitution of
a state should be without its remedy. Such might
by some be thought to be the case, where that supreme body which in such a convention, was one
of the contracting parties, having incorporated itself with that which was the other, no longer sub-
sists to give any new modification to the engagement. Many ways might however be found to
make the requisite alteration, without any depar-
ture from the spirit of the engagement. Although
that body itself which contracted the engagement
be no more, a *larger body* from whence the first is
understood to have derived its title, may still subsist. Let this larger body be consulted. Various
are the ways that might be conceived of doing this,
and that without any disparagement to the dignity
of the subsisting legislature : of doing it, I mean
. to such effect, as that, should the sense of such
larger body be favourable to the alteration, it may
be made by a law, which, in this case, neither
ought to be, nor probably would be, regarded by

CHAP. IV. the body of the people as a breach of the convention [i].

Notion of a
natural limit
to the su-
preme power,
difficult to
eradicate.

XXXVIII. To return for a moment to the lan-

[i] In Great Britain, for instance, suppose it were deemed necessary to make an alteration in the act of Union. If in an article
stipulated in favour of England, there need be no difficulty; so
that there were a majority for the alteration among the English
members, without reckoning the Scotch. The only difficulty
would be with respect to an article stipulated in favour of Scotland; on account, to wit, of the small number of the Scotch members, in comparison with the English. In such a case, it would
be highly expedient, to say no more, for the sake of preserving
the public faith, and to avoid irritating the body of the nation, to
take some method for making the establishment of the new law,
depend upon their sentiments. One such method might be as
follows. Let the new law in question be enacted in the common
form. But let its commencement be deferred to a distant period,
suppose a year or two: let it then, at the end of that period be in
force, unless petitioned against, by persons of such a description,
and in such number as might be supposed fairly to represent the
sentiments of the people in general: persons, for instance, of the
description of those who at the time of the Union, constituted the
body of electors. To put the validity of the law out of dispute, it
would be necessary the fact upon which it was made ultimately
to depend, should be in its nature too notorious to be controverted.
To determine therefore, whether the conditions upon which the
invalidation of it was made to depend, had been complied with, is
what must be left to the simple declaration of some person or persons; for instance the King. I offer this only as a general idea:
and as one amongst many that perhaps might be offered in the
same view. It will not be expected that I should here answer
objections, or enter into details.

guage used by those who speak of the supreme
power as being limited in its own nature. One
thing I would wish to have remembered. What is
here said. of the impropriety, and evil influence of
that kind of discourse, is not intended to convey
the smallest censure on those who use it, as if in-
tentionally accessary to the ill effects it has a tendency to produce. It is rather a misfortune in the
language, than a fault of any person in particular.
The original of it is lost in the darkness of antiquity. We inherited it from our fathers, and
maugre all its inconveniences, are likely, I doubt,
to transmit it to our children.

XXXIX. I cannot look upon this as a mere dis- This not a mere affair of words.
pute of words. I cannot help persuading myself,
that the disputes between contending parties—
between the defenders of a law and the opposers of it,
would stand a much better chance of being adjusted
than at present, were they but explicitly and constantly referred at once to the principle of UTILITY.
The footing on which this principle rests every
dispute, is that of matter of fact; that is, future
fact—the probability of certain future contingen-
cies. Were the debate then conducted under the
auspices of this principle, one of two things would
happen : either men would come to an agreement
concerning that probability, or they would see at
length, after due discussion of the real grounds of

CHAP. IV. the dispute, that no agreement was to be hoped
for.   They would at any rate see clearly and explicitly, the point on which the *disagreement* turned.
The discontented party would then take their resolution to resist or to submit, upon just grounds,
according as it should appear to them worth their
while—according to what should appear to them,
the importance of the matter in dispute—according
to what should appear to them the probability or
improbability of success—*according*, in short, *as the
mischiefs of submission should appear to bear a less,
or a greater ratio to the mischiefs of resistance*.   But
the door to' reconcilement would be much more
open, when they saw that it might be not a mere
affair of passion, but a difference of judgment, and
that, for any thing they could know to the contrary,
a sincere one, that was the ground of quarrel.

The above
notion per-
petuates
wrangling.

XL. All else is but womanish scolding and
childish altercation, which is sure to irritate, and
which never can persuade.—" *I* say, the legislature
" can*not* do this—*I* say, that it *can*.   *I* say, that to
" do this, *exceeds* the bounds of its *authority*—*I*
" say, it does *not*."—It is evident, that a pair of
disputants setting out in this manner, may go on
irritating and perplexing one another for everlast-
ing, without the smallest chance of ever coming to
an agreement.   It is no more than announcing,
and that in an obscure and at the same time a

peremptory and captious manner, their opposite persuasions, or rather affections, on a question of which neither of them sets himself to discuss the grounds. The question of utility, all this while, most probably, is never so much as at all brought upon the carpet: if it be, the language in which it is discussed is sure to be warped and clouded to make it match with the obscure and entangled pattern we have seen.

XLI. On the other hand, had the debate been *The principle of utility puts an end to it.* originally and avowedly instituted on the footing of utility, the parties might at length have come to an agreement; or at least to a visible and explicit issue.—" *I* say, that the mischiefs of the measure " in question are to *such* an amount.—*I* say, *not* so, " but to a *less.*—*I* say, the benefits of it are only to " *such* an amount.—*I* say, *not* so, but to a *greater.*" —This, we see, is a ground of controversy very different from the former. The question is now manifestly a question of conjecture concerning so many future contingent matters of fact: to solve it, both parties then are naturally directed to support their respective persuasions by the only evidence the nature of the case admits of;—the evidence of such *past* matters of fact as appear to be analogous to those contingent *future* ones. Now these *past* facts are almost always numerous: so numerous, that till brought into view for the pur-

CHAP. IV.
The principle
of *utility* puts
an end to it.
pose of the debate, a great proportion of them are what may very fairly have escaped the observation of one of the parties : and it is owing, perhaps, to this and nothing else, that that party is of the persuasion which sets it at variance with the other. Here, then, we have a plain and open road, perhaps, to present reconcilement : at the worst to an intelligible and explicit issue,—that is to such a ground of difference as may, when thoroughly trodden and explored, be found to lead on to reconcilement at the last. Men, let them but once clearly understand one another, will not be long ere they agree. It is the perplexity of ambiguous and sophistical discourse that, while it distracts and eludes the apprehension, stimulates and enflames the passions.

But it is now high time we should return to our Author, from whose text we have been insensibly led astray, by the nicety and intricacy of the question it seemed to offer to our view.

CHAP. V.

DUTY OF THE SUPREME POWER TO MAKE LAWS.

I. WE now come to the last topic touched upon in this digression: a certain " *duty*," which, according to our Author's account, the supreme power lies under :—the *duty of making laws.*

CHAP. V.

Subject of the paragraph examined in the present chapter.

II. " Thus far," says he, " as to the *right* of the " supreme power to make laws; but farther, it is " its *duty* likewise. *For since* the respective mem- " bers are bound to conform themselves to the will " of the state, it is expedient that they *receive* " *directions* from the state declaratory of that its " will. *But since* it is impossible, in so great a " multitude to give injunctions to every particular " man, relative to each particular action, therefore " the state establishes general rules for the per- " petual information and direction of all persons, " in all points, whether of positive or negative " duty. And this, in order that every man may " know what to look upon as his own, what as " another's; what absolute and what relative duties " are required at his hands; what is to be esteemed

The paragraph recited

r

CHAP. V. " honest, dishonest, or indifferent; what degree
" every man retains of his natural liberty; what he
" has given up as the price of the benefits of so-
" ciety; and after what manner each person is to
" moderate the use and exercise of those rights
" which the state assigns him, in order to promote
" and secure the public tranquillity."

The first sentence examined. The most obvious sense of it nugatory.

III. Still as obscure, still as ambiguous as ever.
The " *supreme power*" we may remember, according
" to the definition so lately given of it by our Author, and so often spoken of, is neither more nor
less than the *power to make laws.* Of this power
we are now told that it is its " *duty*" to make laws.
Hence we learn—what?—that it is its " *duty*" to
do what it does; to be, in short, what it is. This
then is what the paragraph now before us, with its
apparatus of " *fors*" and " *buts*," and " *sinces*," is
designed to prove to us. Of this stamp is that
meaning, at least, of the initial sentence, which is
apparent upon the face of it.

The next most obvious extravagant.

IV. Complete the sense of the phrase, " *to make
laws*;" add to it, in this place, what it wants in
order to be an adequate expression of the import
which the preceding paragraph seemed to annex
to it; you have now, for what is mentioned as the
object of the " *duty*," another sense indeed, but a
sense still more untenable than the foregoing.

" Thus far," says our Author (recapitulating what he had been saying before) ", as to the *right* of the " supreme power to make laws."—By this *right*" we saw, in the preceding chapter, was meant, a right to make laws *in all cases whatsoever.* " But further," he now adds, " it is its *duty* likewise." Its *duty* then to do—what? to do the same thing that it was before asserted to be its *right* to do—to make laws in all cases whatsoever: or (to use another word, and that our Author's own, and that applied to the same purpose) that it is its duty to be " *absolute* *." A sort of duty this which will probably be thought rather a singular one.

V. Mean time the observation which, if I con- jecture right, he really had in view to make, is one which seems very just indeed, and of no mean importance, but which is very obscurely expressed, and not very obviously connected with the purpose of what goes before. The duty he here means is a duty, which respects, I take it, not so much the actual *making* of laws, as the taking of proper measures to *spread abroad* the knowledge of whatever laws happen to *have been* made : a duty which (to adopt some of our Author's own words) is conversant, not so much about *issuing* " directions," as about providing that such as *are* issued shall be " *received.*"

A third sense proposed.

* 1 Comm. p. 49.

CHAP. V.

Objection to
the use of the
word "*duty*"
on this occa-
sion.

VI. Mean time to speak of the *duties* of a supreme power;—of a *legislature*, meaning a *supreme*
legislature;—of a set of men acknowledged to be
absolute;—is what, I must own, I am not very
fond of. Not that I would wish the subordinate
part of the community to be a whit less watchful
over their governors, or more disposed to unlimited
submission in point of *conduct*, than if I were to
talk with ever so much peremptoriness of the
" *duties*" of these latter, and of the *rights* which the
former have against them [a]:, what I am afraid of

[a] With this note let no man trouble himself who is not used,
or does not intend to use himself, to what are called *metaphysical*
speculations: in whose estimation the benefit of understanding
clearly what he is speaking of, is not worth the labour.

Duty (politi-
cal).

1. That may be said to be my *duty* to do (understand political
duty) which you (or some other person or persons) have a *right*
to have me made to do. I have then a DUTY *towards* you: you
have a RIGHT as *against* me.

Right (politi-
cal).

2. What you have a right to have me made to do (understand
a political 'right) is that which I am liable, according to law,
upon a requisition made on your behalf, to be *punished* for not
doing.

Punishment a
fundamental
idea.

3. I say *punished*: for without the notion of punishment (that
is of *pain* annexed to an act, and accruing on a certain *account*,
and from a certain *source*) no notion can we have of either *right*
or *duty*.

To *define* or
expound.

4. Now the idea belonging to the word *pain* is a simple one.
To *define* or rather (to speak more generally) to *expound* a word,
is to resolve, or to make a progress towards resolving, the idea
belonging to it into simple ones.

is, running into solœcism and confusion in *dis-* CHAP. V.
course.

5. For expounding the words *duty, right, power, title,* and those other terms of the same stamp that abound so much in ethics and jurisprudence, either I am much-deceived, or the only method by which any instruction can be conveyed, is that which is here exemplified. An exposition framed after this method I would term *paraphrasis.*

Words not to be expounded but by *para-phrasis.*

6. A word may be said to be expounded by *paraphrasis,* when not that *word* alone is translated into other *words,* but some whole *sentence* of which it forms a part is translated into another *sentence;* the words of which latter are expressive of such ideas as are *simple,* or are more immediately resolvable, into simple ones than those of the former. Such are those expressive of *substances* and *simple modes,* in respect of such *abstract* terms as are expressive of what LOCKE has called *mixed modes.* This, in short, is the only method in which any abstract terms can, at the long run, be expounded to any instructive purpose : that is in terms calculated to raise *images* either of *substances* perceived, or of *emotions;—* sources, one or other of which every idea must be drawn from, to be a clear one.

Paraphrasis what

7. The common method of defining—the method *per genus et differentiam,* as logicians call it, will, in many cases, not at all answer the purpose. Among abstract terms we soon come to such as have no *superior genus.* A definition, *per genus et differentiam,* when applied to these, it is manifest, can make no advance : it must either stop short, or turn back, as it were, upon itself, in a *circulate* or a *repetend.*

Definition *per genus et differentiam,* not universally applicable.

8. "Fortitude is a virtue :—Very well :—but what is a virtue? "A virtue is a disposition :"—Good again :—but what is a *dis-position?* "A disposition is a ---;" and there we stop. The fact is, a *disposition* has no *superior genus :* a *disposition* is not a ---, any thing :—this is not the way to give us any notion of what is

Further examples;— *disposition,—estate,—interest,—power.*

CHAP. V.

The proper
sense of it.

VII. I understand, I think, pretty well, what is meant by the word *duty* (political duty) when applied to myself; and I could not persuade myself, I think, to apply it in the same sense in a regular didactic discourse to those whom I am speaking of as my supreme governors. That is my *duty* to do, which I am liable to be *punished*, according to law, if I do not do: this is the original, ordinary, and proper sense of the word *duty* [b].

meant by it. " A *power*," again, " is a *right* :" and what is a *right?* It is a *power*.—An *estate* is an *interest*, says our Author somewhere; where he begins defining an estate :—as well might he have said an *interest* was an *estate*. As well, in short, were it to define in this manner, a conjunction or a preposition. As well were it to say of the preposition *through*, or of the conjunction *because*; a *through* is a---, or a *because* is a---, and so go on defining them.

An imperfec-
tion frequent
in our Au-
thor's me-
thod.

9. Of this stamp, by the bye, are some of his most fundamental definitions; of consequence they must leave the reader where they found him. But of this, perhaps, more fully and methodically on some future occasion. In the mean time I have thrown out these loose hints for the consideration of the curious.

Duties, three
sorts.

[b] 1. One may conceive three sorts of duties; *political, moral,* and *religious;* correspondent to the three sorts of *sanctions* by which they are enforced: or the same point of conduct may be a man's duty on these three several accounts. After speaking of the one of these to put the change upon the reader, and without warning begin speaking of another, or not to let it be seen from the first which of them one is speaking of, cannot but be productive of confusion.

Political
duty.

2. Political duty is created by punishment; or at least by the

Have these supreme governors any such duty? No: CHAP. V.
for if they are at all liable to punishment according *The proper
sense of it.*

will of persons who have punishment in their hands; persons stated
and *certain,*—political superiors.

3. Religious duty is also created by punishment: by punish- *Religious duty.*
ment expected at the hands of a person *certain,*—the Supreme
Being.

4. Moral duty is created by a kind of motive, which from the *Moral duty*
uncertainty of the *persons* to apply it, and of the *species* and *degree*
in which it will be applied, has hardly yet got the name of punishment: by various mortifications resulting from the ill-will of persons uncertain and variable,—the community in general: that is,
such individuals of that community as he, whose duty is in question, shall happen to be connected with.

5. When in any of these three senses a man asserts a point of *Difference between these*
conduct to be a duty, what he asserts is the existence, actual or *senses and a
fourth which*
probable, of an *external* event: viz. of a punishment issuing from *is figurative
and improper.*
one or other of these sources in consequence of a contravention of
the duty: an event *extrinsic* to, and distinct from, as well the
conduct of the party spoken of, as the sentiment of him who
speaks. If he persists in asserting it to be a duty, but without
meaning it should be understood that it is on any one of these
three accounts that he looks upon it as such; all he then asserts
is his own internal *sentiment*: all he means then is, that he feels
himself *pleased* or *displeased* at the thoughts of the point of conduct in question, but without being able to tell *why.* In this case
he should e'en say so: and not seek to give an undue influence
to his own single suffrage, by delivering it in terms that purport
to declare the voice either of God, or of the law, or of the people.

6. Now which of all these senses of the word our Author had *Duty* not ap-
plicable here
in mind; in which of them all he meant to assert that it was the *in any proper
sense.*
duty of supreme governors to make laws, I know not. *Political*

CHAP. V. to law, whether it be for *not* doing any thing, or

The *proper* sense of it.

for *doing*, then are they not, what they are sup-

duty is what they cannot be subject to* : and to say that a duty even of the *moral* or *religious* kind to this effect is incumbent on them, seems rather a precipitate assertion.

In truth what he meant was neither more nor less, I suppose, than that he should be glad to see them do what he *is* speaking of ; to wit, " *make* laws :" that is, as he explains himself, spread abroad the knowledge of them.—Would he so? So indeed should I ; and if asked why, what answer our Author would give I know not; but I, for my part, have no difficulty. I answer,—because I am persuaded that it is for the benefit of the community that they (its governors) should do so. This would be enough to warrant me in my own opinion for saying that they *ought* to do it. For all this, I should not, at any rate, say that it was their *duty* in a *political* sense. No more should I venture to say it was in a *moral* or *religious* sense, till I were satisfied whether they themselves *thought* the measures useful and feasible, and whether they were generally *supposed* to think so.

Were I satisfied that they *themselves* thought so, God then, I might say, knows they do. God, we are to suppose, will punish them if they neglect pursuing it. It is then their *religious* duty. Were I satisfied that the *people* supposed they thought so : the people, I might say, in case of such neglect,—the people, by various manifestations of its ill-will, will also punish them. It is then their *moral* duty.

In any of these senses it must be observed, there can be no more propriety in averring it to be the duty of the supreme power to pursue the measure in question, than in averring it to be their duty to pursue any other supposable measure equally bene-ficial to the community. To usher in the proposal of a measure in this peremptory and assuming guise, may be pardonable in a

* See the note following.

posed to be, supreme governors [c]: those are
the supreme governors, by whose appointment the
former are liable to be punished.

VIII. The word duty, then, if applied to persons
spoken of as supreme governors, is evidently applied to them in a sense which is figurative and
improper: nor therefore are the same conclusions
to be drawn from any propositions in which it is
used in this sense, as might be drawn from them
if it were used in the other sense, which is its
proper one.

*That in which
it is here used
figurative.*

IX. This explanation, then, being premised;—understanding myself to be using the word *duty* in its
improper sense, the proposition that it is the duty
of the legislature to spread abroad, as much as

*The proposi-
tion acceded
to in this last
sense.—*

loose rhetorical harangue, but can never be justifiable in an exact
didactic composition. Modes of *private moral* conduct there are
indeed many, the tendency whereof is so well known and so
generally acknowledged, that the observance of them may well be
stiled a duty. But to apply the same term to the particular details of *legislative* conduct, especially newly proposed ones, is
going, I think, too far, and tends only to confusion.

[c] I mean for what they do, or omit to do, when *acting in a
body*: in that body in which, when acting, they are *supreme*.
Because for any thing any of them do separately, or acting in
bodies that are subordinate, they may any of them be punished
without any disparagement to their supremacy. Not only any
may be, but many *are*: it is what we see examples of every day.

*Governors in
what way sub-
ject to politi-
cal duties
notwith-
standing
their being
supreme.*

CHAP. V. possible, the knowledge of their will among the people, is a proposition I am disposed most unreservedly to accede to. If this be our Author's meaning, I join myself to him heart and voice.

Obscured again by the next sentence —the Censor's part confounded with that of the Historian.

X. What particular institutions our Author wished to see established in this view—what *particular* duties he would have found for the legislature under this *general* head of duty, is not very apparent: though it is what should have appeared more precisely than it does, ere his meaning could be apprehended to any purpose. What encreases still the difficulty of apprehending it, is a practice which we have already had more than once occasion to detect him in *,—a kind of versatility, than which nothing can be more vexatious to a reader who makes a point of entering into the sentiments of his Author. He sets out with the word " *duty*" in his mouth; and, in the character of a *Censor*, with all due gravity begins talking to us of what *ought* to be. 'Tis in the midst of this lecture that our *Proteus* slips aside; puts on the *historian;* gives an insensible turn to the discourse; and without any warning of the change, finishes with telling us what *is*. Between these two points, indeed, the *is*, and the *ought to be*, so opposite as they frequently are in the eyes of other men, that spirit of

* V. supra, ch. II. par. 11. ch. III. par. V. ch. IV. par. 10.

obsequious *quietism* that seems constitutional in
our Author, will scarce ever let him recognize a
difference. 'Tis in the second sentence of the paragraph that he observes that " it is *expedient* that
" they" (the people) " receive directions from the
" state" (meaning the governing body) " declara-
" tory of that it's will."   'Tis in the very next sentence that we learn from him, that what it is thus
" *expedient*" that the state *should* do, it *does* do.
" But since it is impossible in so great a multitude,
" to give particular injunctions to every particular
" man relative to each particular action, therefore,"
says he, " the state establishe*s*" (does *actually*
establish) " general rule*s*" (*the* state generally, *any*
state, that is to say, that one can mention, all
states, in short, whatever *do* establish) " general
" rules for the perpetual information and direction
" of *all* persons in *all* points, whether of positive
" or of negative duty."   Thus far our Author; so
that, for ought appears, whatever he could *wish* to
see done in this view *is* done.   Neither this state
of our own, nor any other, does he wish to see do
any thing more in the matter than he sees done
already; nay, nor than what is sure to be done at
all events : so that happily the duty he is here so
forward to lay on his superiors will not sit on them
very heavy.   Thus far is he from having any determinate instructive meaning in that part of the para-

CHAP. V.

Obscured
again by the
next sentence
---the Cen-
sor's art con-
founded with
that of the
Historian.

CHAP. V. graph in which, to appearance, and by accident, he
comes nearest to it.

—Fixed and
particular-
ised.—*Pro-
mulgation* re-
commended.

XI. Not that the passage however is absolutely
so remote from meaning, but that the inventive
complaisance of a commentator of the admiring
breed might find it pregnant with a good deal of
useful matter. The design of disseminating the
knowledge of the laws is glanced at by it at least,
with a shew of approbation. Were our Author's
writings then as sacred as they are mysterious;
and were they in the number of those which stamp
the seal of authority on whatever doctrines can be
fastened on them; what we have read might serve
as a text, from which the obligation of adopting as
many measures as a man should deem subservient
to that design, might, without any unexampled
violence, be deduced. In this oracular passage I
might find inculcated, if not *totidem syllabis*, at
least *totidem literis*, as many points of legislative
duty as should seem subservient to the purposes of
digestion and *promulgation*. Thus fortified, I might
press upon the legislature, and that on the score of
" *duty*," to carry into execution, and that without
delay, many a busy project as yet either unthought
of or unheeded. I might call them with a tone of
authority to their work: I bid them go make provi-
sion forthwith for the bringing to light such scattered materials as can be found of the judicial decisions

of time past,—sole and neglected materials of common law;—for the registering and publishing of all future ones as they arise;—for transforming, by a digest, the body of the common law thus completed, into statute-law;—for breaking down the whole together into *codes* or parcels, as many as there are classes of persons distinguishably concerned in it; —for introducing to the notice and possession of every person his respective code:—works which public necessity cries aloud for, at which professional interest shudders, and at which legislative indolence[*] stands aghast.

CHAP. V.

—Fixed and particularized.—Promulgation recommended.

XII. All these leading points, I say, of legislative economy, with as many points of detail subservient to each as a meditation not unassiduous has suggested, I might enforce, were it necessary, by our Author's oracular authority. For nothing less than what has been mentioned, I trust, is necessary, in order that every man may be made to know, in the degree in which he *might* and *ought* to be made to know, what (in our Author's words) " to look upon as his own, what as another's; what " absolute and what relative duties are required at " his hands; what is to be esteemed honest, dis- " honest, or indifferent; what degree every man " retains of his natural liberty; what he has given

The recommendation enforced by our Author's concluding sentence.

[*] Had I seen in those days what every body has seen since, instead of *indolence* I should have put *corruption.*—Note of the Author, 1822.

CHAP. V. " up as the price of the benefits of society; and
" after what manner each person is to moderate
" the use and exercise of those rights which the
" state assigns him, in order to promote and secure
" the public tranquillity." In taking my leave of
our Author, I finish gladly with this pleasing pero-
ration: a scrutinizing judgment, perhaps, would
not be altogether satisfied with it; but the ear is
soothed by it, and the heart is warmed.

Necessity
and use of
these verbal
criticisms.

XIII. I now put an end to the tedious and intricate war of words that has subsisted, in a more
particular manner during the course of these two
last chapters: a logomachy, wearisome enough,
perhaps, and insipid to the reader, but beyond
description laborious and irksome to the writer.
What remedy? Had there been sense, I should
have attached myself to the sense: finding nothing
but words; to the words I was to attach myself, or
to nothing. Had the doctrine been but *false*, the
task of exposing it would have been comparatively
an easy one: but it was what is worse, *unmeaning;*
and thence it came to require all these pains which
I have been here bestowing on it: to what profit
let the reader judge.

" Well then,"—(cries an objector)—" the task
" you have set yourself is at an end; and the sub-
" ject of it after all, according to your own repre-
" sentation, teaches nothing;—according to your

" own shewing it is not worth attending to.—Why CHAP. V.

" then bestow on it so much attention?"

In this view—To do something to instruct, but more to undeceive, the timid and admiring student: —to excite him to place more confidence in his own strength, and less in the infallibility of great names : —to help him to emancipate his judgment from the shackles of authority :—to let him see that the not understanding a discourse may as well be the writer's fault as the reader's :—to teach him to distinguish between shewy language and sound sense:— to warn him not to pay himself with words :—to shew him that what may tickle the ear, or dazzle the imagination, will not always inform the judgment :—to shew him what it is our Author can do, and has done; and what it is he has not done, and cannot do:—to dispose him rather to fast on ignorance than feed himself with error:—to let him see that with regard to an expositor of the law, our Author is not *he that should come,* but that we may be still *looking for another.*—" Who then," says my objector, " shall be that other? Yourself?"—No verily.—My mission is at an end, when I have *prepared the way before him.*

FINIS.

T. White & Co. Printers, 14, Bear Alley, London.